CHSPE Preparation Book
2020 – 2021

CHSPE Study Guide and Practice Test Questions for the California High School Proficiency Exam

CHSPE Essential Test Tips DVD

from Trivium Test Prep!

Dear Customer,

Thank you for purchasing from Trivium Test Prep! We're honored to help you prepare for your CHSPE.

To show our appreciation, we're offering a **FREE *CHSPE Essential Test Tips* DVD by Trivium Test Prep**. Our DVD includes 35 test preparation strategies that will make you successful on the CHSPE. All we ask is that you email us your feedback and describe your experience with our product. Amazing, awful, or just so-so: we want to hear what you have to say!

To receive your **FREE *CHSPE Essential Test Tips* DVD**, please email us at 5star@triviumtestprep.com. Include "Free 5 Star" in the subject line and the following information in your email:

1. The title of the product you purchased.

2. Your rating from 1 – 5 (with 5 being the best).

3. Your feedback about the product, including how our materials helped you meet your goals and ways in which we can improve our products.

4. Your full name and shipping address so we can send your FREE *CHSPE Essential Test Tips* DVD.

If you have any questions or concerns please feel free to contact us directly at 5star@triviumtestprep.com.

Thank you!

Table of Contents

Introduction

Congratulations on your decision to take the California High School Proficiency Examination (CHSPE)! This test will assess your competency in high school-level Math, Reading, and Language; if you do well, you may be provided an exemption from high school – at the very least, you'll receive U.S. Department of Education and Federal Student Aid recognition for holding the equivalent of a high school diploma.

But let's not get ahead of ourselves. You've already made a great first step in purchasing this book – the next is to do well on the CHSPE.

What is the CHSPE?

The California High School Proficiency Examination (CHSPE) is a three-and-a-half-hour exam, consisting of three sections: Math, Reading, and Language. The test is open to anyone over the age of sixteen, regardless of whether or not they are currently attending school. (A student under the age of sixteen may still take the CHSPE, but only if they have already completed the 10th grade.)

Anyone who takes and passes the CHSPE is awarded a Certificate of Proficiency from the State Board of Education; this certificate, as mentioned before, is recognized as the equivalent of a high school diploma.

> **Note!** Even if you pass the CHSPE, if you are under the age of eighteen, you are NOT exempt from attending school. If you pass the CHSPE, are under the age of eighteen, and wish to stop attending high school, then you are REQUIRED to have a guardian sign a waiver for you to leave school. More information can be found at the CHSPE website: http://www.chspe.net/about/.

Keep in mind that CHSPE stands for California High School Proficiency Examination. Many states outside of California do NOT recognize the CHSPE as a high school diploma-equivalent. So, if you are applying for college, a federal service job, etc. – that is outside of California – be sure to check out their individual requirements.

The Reading Section

- **54 Questions – Reading Comprehension**: Presents multiple short passages with corresponding questions.

- **30 Questions – Vocabulary**: Tests knowledge of word use and the ability to work with words.

The Language Section

- **48 Questions – Language**: Tests knowledge of basic grammar, punctuation, and sentence structure.

- **Essay**: Requires the composition of a short essay in response to a topic or prompt.

The Math Section

- **50 Questions – Mathematics**: Covers mathematical topics ranging in difficulty from basic operations to algebra and geometry. Requires knowledge of work equations, graphs, measurements and volume, percentages, averages, etc.

Scoring

Your score begins with a "raw" score, indicating how many questions were answered correctly. That raw score is then converted into a scaled score ranging from 250 to 450. (Scores are scaled because of the varying nature of the test. Some tests are more difficult than others; a scaled score balances things out.)

Generally (though again, it varies, so make sure to check whenever you take your test) if you can answer 65% or more of the questions correctly, then you will pass – definitely an attainable goal!

How This Book Works

The subsequent chapters in this book are divided into a review of those topics covered on the exam. This is not intended to "teach" or "re-teach" you these concepts – there is no way to cram all of that material into one book! Instead, we are going to help you recall all of the information which you've already learned. Even more importantly, we'll show you how to apply that knowledge.

Each chapter includes an extensive review, with practice drills at the end to test your knowledge. With time, practice, and determination, you'll be well-prepared for test day.

Chapter 1: Reading Comprehension

The Reading Section of the CHSPE is divided into two parts: Reading Comprehension and Vocabulary. The questions in the Reading Comprehension section are typically not overly difficult, but they do require the reader to pay close attention to every word. Skimming over even one word can completely change the meaning of a sentence, and result in the loss of a point.

There are three types of questions that you can encounter in the Reading Comprehension section of the CHSPE:

1. **About the Author**: The question will ask about the author's attitude, thoughts, opinions, etc. When encountering a question asking specifically about the author, pay attention to context clues in the article. The answer may not be explicitly stated, but instead conveyed in the overall message.

2. **Passage Facts**: You must distinguish between facts and opinions presented in the passage. Remember, a fact is something verifiable or proven, whereas an opinion is simply a belief that cannot be proven for sure. For example: "The sky is blue" is a fact that cannot be argued; "the sky is a prettier blue today than it was yesterday" is an opinion, since there is no scientific basis for what makes the sky "prettier" to a person.

3. **Additional Information**: These questions will have you look at what kind of information could be added to or was missing from the passage. They may also ask in what direction the passage was going. Questions may ask what statement could be added to strengthen the author's statement, or weaken it; they may also provide a fill-in-the-blank option to include a statement that is missing from, but fits with the rest of, the passage. When looking over answer choices, read them with the passage to see if they sound correct in context.

Strategies

Despite the different types of questions you will face, there are some strategies for Reading Comprehension which apply across the board:

- **Read the Answer Choices First**, then read the passage. This will save you time, as you will know what to look out for as you read.

- **Use the Process of Elimination**. Often at least one answer choice in a question is obviously incorrect. After reading the passage, eliminate any blatantly incorrect answer choices to increase your chances of finding the correct answer much more quickly.

- **Avoid "Negatives."** Generally, test-makers will not make negatives statements about anyone or anything. Statements will be either neutral or positive; so if it seems like an answer choice is making a negative connotation, it is very likely that the answer is intentionally false.

Here are some examples of the kinds of questions you may encounter in the Reading Comprehension section. Each passage will have at least one of the above listed question types – try to answer them for yourself before reading the solution. If you run into trouble, don't worry. We'll provide more practice drills later in the book, as well.

Sample One:

Exercise is a critical aspect for healthy development in children. Today, there is an epidemic of unhealthy children in the United States who will face health problems in adulthood due to poor diet and lack of exercise as children. This is a problem for all Americans, especially with the rising cost of health care.

It is vital that school systems and parents encourage their children to engage in a minimum of 30 minutes of cardiovascular exercise each day, meaning their heart rate is mildly increased for sustained period. This is proven to decrease the likelihood of development diabetes, becoming obese, and a multitude of other health problems. Also, children need a proper diet rich in fruits and vegetables so that they can grow and development physically, as well as learn healthy eating habits early on.

1. Which of the following describes the author's use of the word "vital"?
    a) Debatable.
    b) Very important.
    c) Somewhat important.
    d) Not important.
    e) Indicator.

Answer: This is an example of an "About the Author" question. You can tell, from both the tone and the intention of the article, that the author feels very strongly about the health of children and that action should be taken. Therefore, answer **b)** is the correct choice.

2. Which of the following is a fact in the passage, not an opinion?
    a) Fruits and vegetables are the best-tasting foods.
    b) Children today are lazier than they were in previous generations.
    c) The risk of diabetes in children is reduced by physical activity.
    d) Health care costs too much.
    e) Soccer is a better physical activity than tennis.

Answer: A fact is typically presented as a direct statement, not a comparison, which makes answer choice **c)** the correct answer. Notice that many of the incorrect answers contain words that can hint at it being an opinion such as "best," "better," "too much," or other comparisons. Also keep an eye out for answer choices that may be facts, but which are not stated in the passage.

3. What other information might the author have provided to strengthen the argument?
- a) Example of fruits and vegetables children should eat.
- b) How much health insurance costs today vs. 10 years ago.
- c) How many people live in the United States today.
- d) The rules of baseball and soccer.
- e) How many calories the average person burns by running 1 mile.

Answer: All of the choices would provide additional information, but only one pertains specifically to the improvement of health in children: choice **a)**.

Sample Two

Using the below Index, on which page would you find information on Organic Chemistry?

Science
Geology: 110-124
Astronomy: 126-137
Physics: 140-159
Chemistry: 161-170
Biology: 171-179

Math
Geometry: 201-209
Calculus: 210-222
Graphing: 225-251

- a) 210-222
- b) 225-251
- c) 126-137
- d) 161-170
- e) None of the above

Answer: The correct answer is choice **d)**. Pretty simple, huh? These types of questions are the easiest that you will find on the CHSPE. Simply look for key-words (in this case "Chemistry" is the only matching word), and then eliminate everything else that doesn't relate.

REVIEW: READING COMPREHENSION

This section will measure your ability to understand, analyze, and evaluate written passages. The passages will contain material from a variety of sources and will cover a number of different topics.

Strategies

Despite the different types of questions you will face, there are some strategies for Reading Comprehension which apply across the board:

- Read the answer choices first, then read the passage. This will save you time, as you will know what to look out for as you read.

- Use the process of elimination. Some answer choices are obviously incorrect and are relatively easy to detect. After reading the passage, eliminate those blatantly incorrect answer choices; this increases your chance of finding the correct answer much more quickly.

- Avoid negative statements. Generally, test-makers will not make negative statements about anyone or anything. Statements will be either neutral or positive, so if it seems like an answer choice has a negative connotation, it is very likely that the answer is intentionally false.

The Main Idea

The main idea of a text is the purpose behind why a writer would choose to write a book, article, story, etc. Being able to find and understand the main idea is a critical skill necessary to comprehend and appreciate what you're reading.

Consider a political election. A candidate is running for office and plans to deliver a speech asserting her position on tax reform. The **topic** of the speech—tax reform—is clear to voters, and probably of interest to many. However, imagine that the candidate believes that taxes should be lowered. She is likely to assert this argument in her speech, supporting it with examples proving why lowering taxes would benefit the public and how it could be accomplished. While the topic of the speech would be tax reform, the benefit of lowering taxes would be the **main idea**. Other candidates may have different perspectives on the topic; they may believe that higher taxes are necessary, or that current taxes are adequate. It is likely that their speeches, while on the same topic of tax reform, would have different main ideas: different arguments likewise supported by different examples. Determining what a speaker, writer, or text is asserting about a specific issue will reveal the main idea.

One more quick note: the CHSPE may also ask about a passage's **theme**, which is similar to but distinct from its topic. While a topic is usually a specific *person, place, thing,* or *issue,* the theme is an *idea* or *concept* that the author refers back to frequently. Examples of common themes include ideas like the importance of family, the dangers of technology, and the beauty of nature.

There will be many questions on the CHSPE that require you to differentiate between the topic, theme, and main idea of a passage. Let's look at an example passage to see how you would answer these questions.

Example: "Babe Didrikson Zaharias, one of the most decorated female athletes of the twentieth century, is an inspiration for everyone. Born in 1911 in Beaumont, Texas, Zaharias lived in a time when women were considered second-class to men, but she never let that stop her from becoming a champion. Babe was one of seven children in a poor immigrant family, and was competitive from an early age. As a child she excelled at most things she tried, especially sports, which continued into high school and beyond. After high school, Babe played amateur basketball for two years, and soon after began training in track and field. Despite the fact that women were only allowed to enter in three events, Babe represented the United States in the 1932 Los Angeles Olympics, and won two gold medals and one silver for track and field events.

"In the early 1930s, Babe began playing golf which earned her a legacy. The first tournament she entered was a men's only tournament, however she did not make the cut to play. Playing golf as an amateur was the only option for a woman at this time, since there was no professional women's league. Babe played as an amateur for a little over a decade, until she turned pro in 1947 for the Ladies Professional Golf Association (LPGA) of which she was a founding member. During her career as a golfer, Babe won eighty-two tournaments, amateur and professional, including the U.S. Women's Open, All-American Open, and British Women's Open Golf Tournament. In 1953, Babe was diagnosed with cancer, but fourteen weeks later, she played in a tournament. That year she won her third U.S. Women's Open. However by 1955, she didn't have the physicality to compete anymore, and she died of the disease in 1956."

Determining the main idea, however, requires a little more analysis. The passage describes Babe Zaharias' life, but the main idea of the paragraph is what it says about her life. To figure out the main idea, consider what the writer is saying about Babe Zaharias. The writer is saying that she's someone to admire—that's the main idea and what unites all the information in the paragraph. Lastly, what might the theme of the passage be? The writer refers to several broad concepts, including never giving up and overcoming the odds, both of which could be themes for the passage. Two major indicators of the main idea of a paragraph or passage follow below:

- It is a general idea; it applies to all the more specific ideas in the passage. Every other sentence in a paragraph should be able to relate in some way to the main idea.

- It asserts a specific viewpoint that the author supports with facts, opinions, or other details. In other words, the main idea takes a stand.

Example: "From so far away it's easy to imagine the surface of our solar system's planets as enigmas—how could we ever know what those far-flung planets really look like? It turns out, however, that scientists have a number of tools at their disposal that allow them to paint detailed pictures of many planets' surfaces. The topography of Venus, for example, has been explored by several space probes, including the Russian Venera landers and NASA's Magellan orbiter. These craft used imaging and radar to map the surface of the planet, identifying a whole host of features including volcanoes, craters, and a complex system of channels. Mars has similarly been mapped by space probes, including the famous Mars Rovers, which are automated vehicles that actually landed on the surface of Mars. These rovers have been used by NASA and other space agencies to study the geology, climate, and possible biology of the planet.

"In addition these long-range probes, NASA has also used its series of orbiting telescopes to study distant planets. These four massively powerful telescopes include the famous Hubble Space Telescope as well as the Compton Gamma Ray Observatory, Chandra X-Ray Observatory, and the Spitzer Space Telescope. Scientists can use these telescopes to examine planets using not only visible light but also infrared and near-infrared light, ultraviolet light, x-rays and gamma rays.

"Powerful telescopes aren't just found in space: NASA makes use of Earth-bound telescopes as well. Scientists at the National Radio Astronomy Observatory in Charlottesville, VA, have spent decades using radio imaging to build an incredibly detailed portrait of Venus' surface. In fact, Earth-bound telescopes offer a distinct advantage over orbiting telescopes because they allow scientists to capture data from a fixed point, which in turn allows them to effectively compare data collected over long period of time."

Which of the following sentences best describes the main of the passage?
- a) It's impossible to know what the surfaces of other planets are really like.
- b) Telescopes are an important tool for scientists studying planets in our solar system.
- c) Venus' surface has many of the same features as the Earth's, including volcanoes, craters, and channels.
- d) Scientists use a variety of advanced technologies to study the surface of the planets in our solar system.

Answer a) can be eliminated because it directly contradicts the rest of the passage, which goes into detail about how scientists have learned about the surfaces of other planets. Answers b) and c) can also be eliminated because they offer only specific details from the passage—while both choices contain details from the passage, neither is general enough to encompass the passage as a whole. Only answer d) provides an assertion that is both backed up by the passage's content and general enough to cover the entire passage.

Topic and Summary Sentences

The main idea of a paragraph usually appears within the topic sentence. The **topic sentence** introduces the main idea to readers; it indicates not only the topic of a passage, but also the writer's perspective on the topic.

The first sentence in the Babe Zaharias text states the main idea: *Babe Didrikson Zaharias, one of the most decorated female athletes of the twentieth century, is an inspiration for everyone.*

Even though paragraphs generally begin with topic sentences due to their introductory nature, on occasion writers build up to the topic sentence by using supporting details in order to generate interest or build an argument. Be alert for paragraphs when writers do not include a clear topic sentence at all;

even without a clear topic sentence, a paragraph will still have a main idea. You may also see a **summary sentence** at the end of a passage. As its name suggests, this sentence sums up the passage, often by restating the main idea and the author's key evidence supporting it.

Example: In the following paragraph, what are the topic and summary sentences?

"The Constitution of the United States establishes a series of limits to rein in centralized power. Separation of powers distributes federal authority among three competing branches: the executive, the legislative, and the judicial. Checks and balances allow the branches to check the usurpation of power by any one branch. States' rights are protected under the Constitution from too much encroachment by the federal government. Enumeration of powers names the specific and few powers the federal government has. These four restrictions have helped sustain the American republic for over two centuries."

The topic sentence is the first sentence in the paragraph. It introduces the topic of discussion, in this case the constitutional limits aimed at resisting centralized power. The summary sentence is the last sentence in the paragraph. It sums up the information that was just presented: here, that constitutional limits have helped sustain the United States of America for over two hundred years.

Implied Main Idea

When there's no clear topic sentence, you're looking for an **implied main idea**. This requires some detective work: you will need to look at the author's word choice and tone in addition to the content of the passage to find his or her main idea. Let's look at an example paragraph.

Example: "One of my summer reading books was *Mockingjay*. Though it's several hundred pages long, I read it in just a few days *I was captivated by the adventures of the main character and the complicated plot of the book. However, I felt like the ending didn't reflect the excitement of the story. Given what a powerful personality the main character has, I felt like the ending didn't do her justice.*"

Even without a clear topic sentence, this paragraph has a main idea. What is the writer's perspective on the book—what is the writer saying about it?
  a) *Mockingjay* is a terrific novel.
  b) *Mockingjay* is disappointing.
  c) *Mockingjay* is full of suspense.
  d) *Mockingjay* is a lousy novel.

The correct answer is B): the novel is disappointing. The process of elimination will reveal the correct answer if that is not immediately clear. While that the paragraph begins with positive commentary on the book—*I was captivated by the adventures of the main character and the complicated plot of the book*—this positive idea is followed by the contradictory transition word *however*. A) cannot be the correct answer because the author concludes that the novel was poor. Likewise, D) cannot be correct because it does not encompass all the ideas in the paragraph; despite the negative conclusion, the author enjoyed most of the book.

The main idea should be able to encompass all of the thoughts in a paragraph; choice D) does not apply to the beginning of this paragraph. Finally, choice C) is too specific; it could only apply to the brief description of the plot and adventures of the main character. That leaves choice B) as the best option. The author initially enjoyed the book, but was disappointed by the ending, which seemed unworthy of the exciting plot and character.

Example: "Fortunately, none of Alyssa's coworkers has ever seen inside the large filing drawer in her desk. Disguised by the meticulous neatness of the rest of her workspace, there was no sign of the chaos beneath. To even open it, she had to struggle for several minutes with the enormous pile of junk jamming the drawer, until it would suddenly give way, and papers, folders, and candy wrappers spilled out of the top and onto the floor. It was an organizational nightmare, with torn notes and spreadsheets haphazardly thrown on top of each other, and melted candy smeared across pages. She was worried the odor would soon permeate to her coworker's desks, revealing to them her secret."

Which sentence best describes the main idea of the paragraph above?
  a) Alyssa wishes she could move to a new desk.
  b) Alyssa wishes she had her own office.
  c) Alyssa is glad none of her coworkers know about her messy drawer.
  d) Alyssa is sad because she doesn't have any coworkers.

Clearly, Alyssa has a messy drawer, and C) is the right answer. The paragraph begins by indicating her gratitude that her coworkers do not know about her drawer (*Fortunately, none of Alyssa's coworkers has ever seen inside the large filing drawer in her desk.*) Plus, notice how the drawer is described: *it was an organizational nightmare*, and it apparently doesn't even function properly: *to even open the drawer, she had to struggle for several minutes.* The writer reveals that it has an odor, with *melted candy* inside. Alyssa is clearly ashamed of her drawer and fearful of being judged by her coworkers for it.

Supporting Details

Supporting details provide more support for the author's main idea. For instance, in the Babe Zaharias example above, the writer makes the general assertion that *Babe Didrikson Zaharias, one of the most decorated female athletes of the twentieth century, is an inspiration for everyone.* The rest of the paragraph provides supporting details with facts showing why she is an inspiration: the names of the illnesses she overcame, and the specific years she competed in the Olympics.

Be alert for **signal words**, which can be helpful in identifying supporting details. Signal words can also help you rule out sentences that are too broad to be the main idea or topic sentence: if a sentence begins with a signal word, it will likely be too specific to be a main idea.

Questions on the CHSPE will ask you to do two things with supporting details: you will need to find details that support a particular idea and also explain why a particular detail was included in the passage. In order to answer these questions, you need to have a solid understanding of the passage's main idea. With this knowledge, you can determine how a supporting detail fits in with the larger structure of the passage.

Example: "From so far away it's easy to imagine the surface of our solar system's planets as enigmas—how could we ever know what those far-flung planets really look like? It turns out, however, that scientists have a number of tools at their disposal that allow them to paint detailed pictures of many planets' surfaces. The topography of Venus, for example, has been explored by several space probes, including the Russian *Venera* landers and NASA's *Magellan* orbiter. These craft used imaging and radar to map the surface of the planet, identifying a whole host of features including volcanoes, craters, and a complex system of channels. Mars has similarly been mapped by space probes, including the famous Mars Rovers, which are automated vehicles that actually landed on the surface of Mars. These rovers have been used by NASA and other space agencies to study the geology, climate, and possible biology of the planet.

"In addition these long-range probes, NASA has also used its series of orbiting telescopes to study distant planets. These four massively powerful telescopes include the famous Hubble Space Telescope as well as the Compton Gamma Ray Observatory, Chandra X-Ray Observatory, and the Spitzer Space Telescope. Scientists can use these telescopes to examine planets using not only visible light but also infrared and near-infrared light, ultraviolet light, x-rays and gamma rays. Powerful telescopes aren't just found in space: NASA makes use of Earth-bound telescopes as well. Scientists at the National Radio Astronomy Observatory in Charlottesville, VA, have spent decades using radio imaging to build an incredibly detailed portrait of Venus' surface. In fact, Earth-bound telescopes offer a distinct advantage over orbiting telescopes because they allow scientists to capture data from a fixed point, which in turn allows them to effectively compare data collected over long period of time."

Which sentence from the text best helps develop the idea that scientists make use of many different technologies to study the surfaces of other planets?
> a) These rovers have been used by NASA and other space agencies to study the geology, climate, and possible biology of the planet.
> b) From so far away it's easy to imagine the surface of our solar system's planets as enigmas—how could we ever know what those far-flung planets really look like?
> c) In addition these long-range probes, NASA has also used its series of orbiting telescopes to study distant planets.
> d) These craft used imaging and radar to map the surface of the planet, identifying a whole host of features including volcanoes, craters, and a complex system of channels.

You're looking for detail from the passage that supports the main idea—scientists make use of many different technologies to study the surfaces of other planets. Answer a) includes a specific detail about rovers, but does not offer any details that support the idea of multiple technologies being used. Similarly, answer d) provides another specific detail about space probes. Answer b) doesn't provide any supporting details; it simply introduces the topic of the passage. Only answer c) provides a detail that directly supports the author's assertion that scientists use multiple technologies to study the planets.

If true, which detail could be added to the passage above to support the author's argument that scientists use many different technologies to study the surface of planets?

a) Because the Earth's atmosphere blocks x-rays, gamma rays, and infrared radiation, NASA needed to put telescopes in orbit above the atmosphere.
b) In 2015, NASA released a map of Venus which was created by compiling images from orbiting telescopes and long-range space probes.
c) NASA is currently using the *Curiosity* and *Opportunity* rovers to look for signs of ancient life on Mars.
d) NASA has spent over $2.5 billion to build, launch, and repair the Hubble Space Telescope.

You can eliminate answers c) and d) because they don't address the topic of studying the surface of planets. Answer a) can also be eliminated because it only addresses a single technology. Only choice b) provides would add support to the author's claim about the importance of using multiple technologies.

The author likely included the detail *Earth-bound telescopes offer a distinct advantage over orbiting telescopes because they allow scientists to capture data from a fixed point* in order to:
a) Explain why it has taken scientists so long to map the surface of Venus.
b) Suggest that Earth-bound telescopes are the most important equipment used by NASA scientists.
c) Prove that orbiting telescopes will soon be replaced by Earth-bound telescopes.
d) Demonstrate why NASA scientists rely on my different types of scientific equipment.

Only answer d) directs directly to the author's main argument. The author doesn't mention how long it has taken to map the surface of Venus (answer a), nor does he say that one technology is more important than the others (answer b). And while this detail does highlight the advantages of using Earth-bound telescopes, the author's argument is that many technologies are being used at the same time, so there's no reason to think that orbiting telescopes will be replaced (answer c).

Text Structure

Authors can structure passages in a number of different ways. These distinct organizational patterns, referred to as **text structure**, use the logical relationships between ideas to improve the readability and coherence of a text. The most common ways passages are organized include:

- **problem-solution**: the author presents a problem and then discusses a solution

- **comparison-contrast**: the author presents two situations and then discusses the similarities and differences

- **cause-effect**: the author presents an action and then discusses the resulting effects

- **descriptive**: an idea, object, person, or other item is described in detail

Example: "The issue of public transportation has begun to haunt the fast-growing cities of the southern United States. Unlike their northern counterparts, cities like Atlanta, Dallas, and

Houston have long promoted growth out and not up—these are cities full of sprawling suburbs and single-family homes, not densely concentrated skyscrapers and apartments. What to do then, when all those suburbanites need to get into the central business districts for work? For a long time it seemed highways were the answer: twenty-lane wide expanses of concrete that would allow commuters to move from home to work and back again. But these modern miracles have become time-sucking, pollution spewing nightmares. They may not like it, but it's time for these cities to turn toward public transport like trains and buses if they want their cities to remain livable."

The organization of this passage can best be described as:
      a) a comparison of two similar ideas
      b) a description of a place
      c) a discussion of several effects all related to the same cause
      d) a discussion of a problem followed by the suggestion of a solution

You can exclude answer choice c) because the author provides no root cause or a list of effects. From there this question gets tricky, because the passage contains structures similar to those described above. For example, it compares two things (cities in the North and South) and describes a place (a sprawling city). However, if you look at the overall organization of the passage, you can see that it starts by presenting a problem (transportation) and then presents a solution (trains and buses), making answer d) the only choice that encompasses the entire passage.

The Author's Purpose

Whenever an author writes a text, she always has a purpose, whether that's to entertain, inform, explain, or persuade. A short story, for example, is meant to entertain, while an online news article would be designed to inform the public about a current event.

Each of these different types of writing has a specific name. On the CHSPE, you will be asked to identify which of these categories a passage fits into:

- **Narrative writing** tells a story. (novel, short story, play)

- **Expository writing** informs people. (newspaper and magazine articles)

- **Technical writing** explains something. (product manual, directions)

- **Persuasive writing** tries to convince the reader of something. (opinion column on a blog)

You may also be asked about primary and secondary sources. These terms describe not the writing itself but the author's relationship to what's being written about. A **primary source** is an unaltered piece of writing that was composed during the time when the events being described took place; these texts are often written by the people involved. A **secondary source** might address the same topic but provides extra commentary or analysis. These texts can be written by people not directly involved in the events. For example, a book written by a political candidate to inform people about his or her stand on an issue is a primary source; an online article written by a journalist analyzing how that position will affect the election is a secondary source.

Example: "Elizabeth closed her eyes and braced herself on the armrests that divided her from her fellow passengers. Take-off was always the worst part for her. The revving of the engines, the way her stomach dropped as the plane lurched upward: it made her feel sick. Then, she had to watch the world fade away beneath her, getting smaller and smaller until it was just her and the clouds hurtling through the sky. Sometimes (but only sometimes) it just had to be endured, though. She focused on the thought of her sister's smiling face and her new baby nephew as the plane slowly pulled onto the runway."

The passage above is reflective of which type of writing?
    a) Narrative
    b) Expository
    c) Technical
    d) Persuasive

The passage is telling a story—we meet Elizabeth and learn about her fear of flying—so it's a narrative text (answer a). There is no factual information presented or explained, nor is the author trying to persuade the reader.

Facts vs. Opinions

On the CHSPE Reading passages you might be asked to identify a statement in a passage as either a fact or an opinion, so you'll need to know the difference between the two. A **fact** is a statement or thought that can be proven to be true. The statement *Wednesday comes after Tuesday* is a fact—you can point to a calendar to prove it. In contrast, an **opinion** is an assumption that is not based in fact and cannot be proven to be true. The assertion that *television is more entertaining than feature films* is an opinion—people will disagree on this, and there's no reference you can use to prove or disprove it.

Example: "Exercise is critical for healthy development in children. Today, there is an epidemic of unhealthy children in the United States who will face health problems in adulthood due to poor diet and lack of exercise as children. This is a problem for all Americans, especially with the rising cost of healthcare.
"It is vital that school systems and parents encourage their children to engage in a minimum of thirty minutes of cardiovascular exercise each day, mildly increasing their heart rate for a sustained period. This is proven to decrease the likelihood of developmental diabetes, obesity, and a multitude of other health problems. Also, children need a proper diet rich in fruits and vegetables so that they can grow and develop physically, as well as learn healthy eating habits early on."

Which of the following is a fact in the passage, not an opinion?
    a) Fruits and vegetables are the best way to help children be healthy.
    b) Children today are lazier than they were in previous generations.

c) The risk of diabetes in children is reduced by physical activity.

d) Children should engage in thirty minutes of exercise a day.

Choice b) can be discarded immediately because it is negative and is not discussed anywhere in the passage. Answers a) and d) are both opinions—the author is promoting exercise, fruits, and vegetables as a way to make children healthy. (Notice that these incorrect answers contain words that hint at being an opinion such as *best*, *should*, or other comparisons.) Answer b), on the other hand, is a simple fact stated by the author; it's introduced by the word *proven* to indicate that you don't need to just take the author's word for it.

Drawing Conclusions

In addition to understanding the main idea and factual content of a passage, you'll also be asked to take your analysis one step further and anticipate what other information could logically be added to the passage. In a non-fiction passage, for example, you might be asked which statement the author of the passage would agree with. In an excerpt from a fictional work, you might be asked to anticipate what the character would do next.

To answer these questions, you need to have a solid understanding of the topic, theme, and main idea of the passage; armed with this information, you can figure out which of the answer choices best fits within those criteria (or alternatively, which ones do not). For example, if the author of the passage is advocating for safer working conditions in textile factories, any supporting details that would be added to the passage should support that idea. You might add sentences that contain information about the number of accidents that occur in textile factories or that outline a new plan for fire safety.

Example: "Today, there is an epidemic of unhealthy children in the United States who will face health problems in adulthood due to poor diet and lack of exercise during their childhood. This is a problem for all Americans, as adults with chronic health issues are adding to the rising cost of healthcare. A child who grows up living an unhealthy lifestyle is likely to become an adult who does the same.

"Because exercise is critical for healthy development in children, it is vital that school systems and parents encourage their children to engage in a minimum of thirty minutes of cardiovascular exercise each day. Even this small amount of exercise has been proven to decrease the likelihood that young people will develop diabetes, obesity, and other health issues as adults. In addition to exercise, children need a proper diet rich in fruits and vegetables so that they can grow and develop physically. Starting a good diet early also teaches children healthy eating habits they will carry into adulthood."

The author of this passage would most likely agree with which statement?
   a) Parents are solely responsible for the health of their children.
   b) Children who do not want to exercise should not be made to.
   c) Improved childhood nutrition will help lower the amount Americans spend on healthcare.
   d) It's not important to teach children healthy eating habits because they will learn them as adults.

The author would most likely support answer c): he mentions in the first paragraph that unhealthy habits are adding to the rising cost of healthcare. The main idea of the passage is that nutrition and exercise are important for children, so answer b) doesn't make sense—the author would likely support measures to encourage children to exercise. Answers a) and d) can also be eliminated because they are directly contradicted in the text. The author specifically mentions the role of schools systems, so he doesn't believe parents are solely responsible for their children's health. He also specifically states that children who grow up with unhealthy habit will become adults with unhealthy habits, which contradicts d).

Example: "Elizabeth closed her eyes and braced herself on the armrests that divided her from her fellow passengers. Take-off was always the worst part for her. The revving of the engines, the way her stomach dropped as the plane lurched upward: it made her feel sick. Then, she had to watch the world fade away beneath her, getting smaller and smaller until it was just her and the clouds hurtling through the sky. Sometimes (but only sometimes) it just had to be endured, though. She focused on the thought of her sister's smiling face and her new baby nephew as the plane slowly pulled onto the runway."

Which of the following is Elizabeth least likely to do in the future?
   a) Take a flight to her brother's wedding.
   b) Apply for a job as a flight attendant.
   c) Never board an airplane again.
   d) Get sick on an airplane.

It's clear from the passage that Elizabeth hates flying, but it willing to endure it for the sake of visiting her family. Thus, it seems likely that she would be willing to get on a plane for her brother's wedding, making a) and c) incorrect answers. The passage also explicitly tells us that she feels sick on planes, so d) is likely to happen. We can infer, though, that she would not enjoy being on an airplane for work, so she's very unlikely to apply for a job as a flight attendant, which is choice b).

Test Your Knowledge: Reading Comprehension

Remember to read the questions first, make sure that you read ALL answer choices ALL THE WAY THROUGH, and use process of elimination to make your job of selecting the correct answer easier. If you can answer a majority of these questions correctly, you are likely ready for the Reading Section of the CHSPE.

Read each of the following paragraphs carefully and answer the questions that follow.

Passage 1: The Flu

Influenza, or the flu, has historically been one of the most common and deadliest human sicknesses. While many people who contract this virus will recover, others will not. Over the past 150 years, tens of millions of people have died from the flu, and millions more have been left with lingering complications including secondary infections.

Although it's a common disease, the flu is actually not highly infectious; that is, it is relatively difficult to contract. The virus can only be transmitted when individuals come into direct contact with the bodily fluids of people infected with it, often when they are exposed to expelled aerosol particles resulting from coughing and sneezing. Since these particles only travel short distances and the virus will die within a few hours on hard surfaces, it can be contained with simple health measures like hand washing and face masks.

However, the spread of this disease can only be contained when people are aware that such measures must be taken. One of the reasons the flu has historically been so deadly is the window of time between a person's infection and the development of symptoms. Viral shedding—when the body releases a virus that has been successfully reproducing in it—takes place two days after infection, while symptoms do not usually develop until the third day. Thus, infected individuals may unknowingly infect others for least twenty-four hours before developing symptoms themselves.

1. What is the main idea of the passage?
    a) The flu is a deadly disease that's difficult to control because people become infectious before they show symptoms.
    b) In order for the flu to be transmitted, individuals must come in contact with bodily fluids from infected individuals.
    c) The spread of flu is easy to contain because the virus does not live long either as aerosol particles or on hard surfaces.
    d) The flu has killed tens of millions of people and can often cause deadly secondary infections.

2. Why isn't the flu considered to be highly infectious?
    a) Many people who get the flu will recover and have no lasting complications, so only a small number of people who become infected will die.
    b) The process of viral shedding takes two days, so infected individuals have enough time to implement simple health measures that stop the spread of the disease.

c) The flu virus cannot travel far or live for long periods of time outside the human body, so its spread can easily be contained if measures are taken.

d) Twenty-four hours is a relatively short period of time for the virus to spread among a population.

3. Which of the following correctly describes the flu?
   a) The flu is easy to contract and always fatal.
   b) The flu is difficult to contract and always fatal.
   c) The flu is easy to contract and sometimes fatal.
   d) The flu is difficult to contract and sometimes fatal.

4. Which statement is not a detail from the passage?
   e) Tens of millions of people have been killed by the flu virus.
   f) There is typically a twenty-four hour window during which individuals are infectious but not showing flu symptoms.
   g) Viral shedding is the process by which people recover from the flu.
   h) The flu can be transmitted by direct contact with bodily fluids from infected individuals or by exposure to aerosol particles.

5. What is the meaning of the word *measures* in the last paragraph?
   a) a plan of action
   b) a standard unit
   c) an adequate amount
   d) a rhythmic movement

6. What can the reader conclude from the passage above?
   a) Preemptively implementing health measures like hand washing and face masks could help stop the spread of the flu virus.
   b) Doctors are not sure how the flu virus is transmitted, so they are unsure how to stop it from spreading.
   c) The flu is dangerous because it is both deadly and highly infectious.
   d) Individuals stop being infectious three days after they are infected.

Passage 2: Snakes

Skin coloration and markings play an important role in the world of snakes. Those intricate diamonds, stripes, and swirls help these animals hide from predators and attract mates. Perhaps most importantly (for us humans, anyway), the markings can also indicate whether a snake is venomous. While it might seem counterintuitive for a poisonous snake to stand out in bright red or blue, that fancy costume tells any approaching predator that eating it would be a bad idea.

If you see a flashy-looking snake out the woods, though, those markings don't necessarily mean it's poisonous: some snakes have a found a way to ward off predators without the actual venom. The California king snake, for example, has very similar markings to the venomous coral snake with whom it frequently shares a habitat. However, the king snake is actually nonvenomous; it's merely pretending to be dangerous to eat. A predatory hawk or eagle, usually hunting from high in the sky, can't tell the difference between the two species, so the king snake gets passed over and lives another day.

7. What is the author's primary purpose in writing this essay?
    a) to explain how the markings on a snake are related to whether it is venomous
    b) to teach readers the difference between coral snakes and king snakes
    c) to illustrate why snakes are dangerous
    d) to demonstrate how animals survive in difficult environments

8. What can the reader conclude from the passage above?
    a) The king snake is dangerous to humans.
    b) The coral snake and the king snake are both hunted by the same predators.
    c) It's safe to handle snakes in the woods because you can easily tell whether they're poisonous.
    d) The king snake changes its markings when hawks or eagles are close by.

9. What is the best summary of this passage?
    a) Humans can use coloration and markings to determine whether snakes are poisonous.
    b) Animals often use coloration and markings to attract mates and warn predators that they're poisonous.
    c) The California king snake and coral snake have nearly identical markings.
    d) Venomous snakes often have bright markings, although nonvenomous snakes can also mimic those colors.

10. Which statement is not a detail from the passage?
    a) Predators will avoid eating king snakes because their markings are similar to those on coral snakes.
    b) King snakes and coral snakes live in the same habitats.
    c) The coral snake uses its coloration to hide from predators.
    d) The king snake is not venomous.

11. What is the meaning of the word *intricate* in the first paragraph?
    a) complicated
    b) colorful
    c) purposeful
    d) changeable

12. What is the difference between king snakes and coral snakes according to the passage?
    a) Both king snakes and coral snakes are nonvenomous, but coral snakes have colorful markings.
    b) Both king snakes and coral snakes are venomous, but king snakes have colorful markings.
    c) King snakes are nonvenomous, while coral snakes are venomous.
    d) Coral snakes are nonvenomous, while king snakes are venomous.

Passage 3: Popcorn

Popcorn is often associated with fun and festivities, both in and out of the home. We eat it in theaters, smothering it in butter, and at home, fresh from the microwave. But popcorn isn't just for fun—it's also a multimillion-dollar industry with a long and fascinating history.

While popcorn might seem like a modern invention, its history actually dates back thousands of years, making it one of the oldest snack foods enjoyed around the world. Popping is believed by food historians to be one of the earliest uses of cultivated corn. In 1948, Herbert Dick and Earle Smith discovered old popcorn dating back 4000 years in the New Mexico Bat Cave. For the Aztecs who called the caves home, popcorn (or *momochitl)* played an important role in society, both as a food staple and in ceremonies. The Aztecs cooked popcorn by heating sand in a fire; when it was heated, kernels were added and would pop when exposed to the heat of the sand.

The American love affair with popcorn began in 1912, when it was first sold in theaters. The popcorn industry flourished during the Great Depression by advertising popcorn as a wholesome and economical food. Selling for five to ten cents a bag, it was a luxury that the downtrodden could afford. With the introduction of mobile popcorn machines at the World's Columbian Exposition, popcorn moved from the theater into fairs and parks. Popcorn continued to rule the snack food kingdom until the rise in popularity of home televisions during the 1950s.

The popcorn industry quickly reacted to its decline in sales by introducing pre-popped and un-popped popcorn for home consumption. However, it wasn't until microwave popcorn became commercially available in 1981 that at-home popcorn consumption began to grow exponentially. With the wide availability of microwaves in the United States, popcorn also began popping up in offices and hotel rooms. The home still remains the most popular popcorn eating spot, though: today, seventy percent of the sixteen billion quarts of popcorn consumed annually in the United States is eaten at home.

13. What can the reader conclude from the passage above?
    a) People ate less popcorn in the 1950s than in previous decades because they went to the movies less.
    b) Without mobile popcorn machines, people would not have been able to eat popcorn during the Great Depression.
    c) People enjoyed popcorn during the Great Depression because it was a luxury food.
    d) During the 1800s, people began abandoning theaters to go to fairs and festivals.

14. What is the author's primary purpose in writing this essay?
    a) to explain how microwaves affected the popcorn industry
    b) to show that popcorn, while popular in American history, is older than many people realize
    c) to illustrate the global history of popcorn from ancient cultures to modern times
    d) to demonstrate the importance of popcorn in various cultures

15. Which of the following is not a fact stated in the passage?
   a) Archaeologists have found popcorn dating back 4000 years.
   b) Popcorn was first sold in theatres in 1912.
   c) Consumption of popcorn dropped in 1981 with the growth in popularity of home televisions.
   d) Seventy percent of the popcorn consumed in the United States is eaten in homes.

16. What is the best summary of this passage?
   a) Popcorn is a popular snack food that dates back thousands of years. Its popularity in the United States has been tied to the development of theatres and microwaves.
   b) Popcorn has been a popular snack food for thousands of years. Archaeologists have found evidence that many ancient cultures used popcorn as a food staple and in ceremonies.
   c) Popcorn was first introduced in America in 1912, and its popularity has grown exponentially since then. Today, over sixteen billion quarts of popcorn are consumed in the United States annually.
   d) Popcorn is a versatile snack food that can be eaten with butter and other toppings. It can also be cooked in a number of different ways, including in microwaves.

Test Your Knowledge: Reading Comprehension – Answers

1. **a)**

2. **c)**

3. **d)**

4. **c)**

5. **a)**

6. **a)**

7. **a)**

8. **b)**

9. **d)**

10. **c)**

11. **a)**

12. **c)**

13. **a)**

14. **b)**

15. **c)**

16. **a)**

Chapter 2: Vocabulary

The next part of the Reading Section of the CHSPE is the Vocabulary section, which will consist of 30 multiple choice questions. These questions will require you to choose: the proper definition of a word (or words) in a sentence; the best description of how a word relates to the sentence; or the word that best belongs in a sentence.

The good news is that you have been answering these types of questions since you first learned to read and write. Different forms of sentence completion questions are used for tests and quizzes in all subject areas, which is one of the reasons they are used on the CHSPE. Don't worry - you won't be expected to know every word in the English language, but you are expected to know a good percentage of commonly-tested words.

Strategies

1. Read the sentence through entirely and say "blank" when you come upon a blank in the sentence. This will give you, not only a feel of the language being used, but the chance to identify any context clues which may help identify the correct choice. We'll go over context clues later in the review.

2. Don't memorize lists of vocabulary. Most students will simply study thousands of new words and their definitions – this is a huge mistake! The test will not provide a list of words and their definitions to match. You will be tested on how words are *used* within a sentence.

   It's important to study in the way you will be tested. Therefore, in order to maximize your score, practice using the words you are learning in sentences, whether by writing and/or conversing with them (doing both is highly recommended). That way, the words will become familiar to you.

   One way to study for this section is to write down 20 new words at the beginning of the week. By the end of the week, you must use all the words on the list in a comprehensive paragraph. (This also helps with the writing section.)

3. Learn the meanings of common word prefixes, suffixes, and root words. We'll review these as well.

4. Read the sentence and answer choices carefully. Just as with reading comprehension, a single detail in a sentence can completely change the meaning.

5. Reread the sentence with your answer choice; does it sound right?

6. If you are still unsure, try to narrow down a couple of answer choices through the process of elimination. Then, make an educated guess.

REVIEW: VOCABULARY

Meaning of Words and Phrases

On the Reading section you may also be asked to provide definitions or intended meanings for words within passages. You may have never encountered some of these words before the test, but there are tricks you can use to figure out what they mean.

Context Clues

The most fundamental vocabulary skill is using the context in which a word is used to determine its meaning. Your ability to observe sentences closely is extremely useful when it comes to understanding new vocabulary words.

There are two types of context that can help you understand the meaning of unfamiliar words: situational context and sentence context. Regardless of which context is present, these types of questions are not really testing your knowledge of vocabulary; rather, they test your ability to comprehend the meaning of a word through its usage.

Situational context is context that is presented by the setting or circumstances in which a word or phrase occurs. **Sentence context** occurs within the specific sentence that contains the vocabulary word. To figure out words using sentence context clues, you should first determine the most important words in the sentence.

There are four types of clues that can help you understand context, and therefore the meaning of a word:

- **Restatement** clues occur when the definition of the word is clearly stated in the sentence.

- **Positive/negative clues** can tell you whether a word has a positive or negative meaning.

- **Contrast clues** include the opposite meaning of a word. Words like *but, on the other hand,* and *however* are tip-offs that a sentence contains a contrast clue.

- **Specific detail clues** provide a precise detail that can illuminate the word's meaning.

It is important to remember that more than one of these clues can be present in the same sentence. The more there are, the easier it will be to determine the meaning of the word. For example, the following sentence uses both restatement and positive/negative clues: *Janet suddenly found herself destitute, so poor she could barely afford to eat.* The second part of the sentence clearly indicates that *destitute* is a negative word. It also restates the meaning: very poor.

Example: I had a hard time reading her *illegible* handwriting.
a) neat
b) unsafe
c) sloppy
d) educated

Already, you know that this sentence is discussing something that is hard to read. Look at the word that *illegible* is describing: handwriting. Based on context clues, you can tell that *illegible* means that her handwriting is hard to read.

Next, look at the answer choices. Choice a), *neat,* is obviously a wrong answer because neat handwriting would not be difficult to read. Choices b) and d), *unsafe* and *educated,* don't make sense. Therefore, choice c), *sloppy,* is the best answer.

Example: The dog was *dauntless* in the face of danger, braving the fire to save the girl trapped inside the building.
a) difficult
b) fearless
c) imaginative
d) startled

Demonstrating bravery in the face of danger would be b) *fearless.* In this case, the restatement clue (*braving the fire*) tells you exactly what the word means.

Example: Beth did not spend any time preparing for the test, but Tyrone kept a *rigorous* study schedule.
a) strict
b) loose
c) boring
d) strange

In this case, the contrast word *but* tells us that Tyrone studied in a different way than Beth, which means it's a contrast clue. If Beth did not study hard, then Tyrone did. The best answer, therefore, is choice a).

Analyzing Words

As you no doubt know, determining the meaning of a word can be more complicated than just looking in a dictionary. A word might have more than one **denotation**, or definition; which one the author intends can only be judged by looking at the surrounding text. For example, the word *quack* can refer to the sound a duck makes, or to a person who publicly pretends to have a qualification which he or she does not actually possess.

A word may also have different **connotations**, which are the implied meanings and emotion a word evokes in the reader. For example, a cubicle is a simply a walled desk in an office, but for many the word implies a constrictive, uninspiring workplace. Connotations can vary greatly between cultures and even between individuals.

Lastly, authors might make use of **figurative language**, which is the use of a word to imply something other than the word's literal definition. This is often done by comparing two things. If you say *I felt like a butterfly when I got a new haircut*, the listener knows you don't resemble an insect but instead felt beautiful and transformed.

Word Structure

Although you are not expected to know every word in the English language for your test, you will need the ability to use deductive reasoning to find the choice that is the best match for the word in question, which is why we are going to explain how to break a word into its parts to determine its meaning. Many words can be broken down into three main parts:

prefix – root – suffix

Roots are the building blocks of all words. Every word is either a root itself or has a root. Just as a plant cannot grow without roots, neither can vocabulary, because a word must have a root to give it meaning. The root is what is left when you strip away all the prefixes and suffixes from a word. For example, in the word *unclear*, if you take away the prefix *un-*, you have the root *clear*.

Roots are not always recognizable words, because they generally come from Latin or Greek words, such as *nat*, a Latin root meaning born. The word *native*, which means a person born in a referenced placed, comes from this root, so does the word *prenatal*, meaning before birth. It's important to keep in mind, however, that roots do not always match the exact definitions of words, and they can have several different spellings.

A **Prefix** is a syllable(s) added to the beginning of a word, while **suffixes** are syllables added to the end of the word. Both carry assigned meanings and can be attached to a word to completely change the word's meaning or to enhance the word's original meaning.

The word *prefix* itself can serve as an example: *fix* means to place something securely and *pre-* means before. Therefore, *prefix* means to place something before or in front. Now let's look at a suffix: in the word *feminism*, *femin* is a root which means female. The suffix *-ism* means act, practice, or process. Thus, *feminism* is the process of establishing equal rights for women.

Although you cannot determine the meaning of a word by a prefix or suffix alone, you can use this knowledge to eliminate answer choices; understanding if a word has a positive or negative connotation can give you the partial meaning of the word.

Antonyms and Synonyms

Antonyms are words that mean either the opposite or almost the opposite meaning of the word in question. Synonyms are, interestingly enough, the antonyms of the word antonym. These are words that mean either the same thing or almost the same thing as the word in question.

On the CHSPE, you will be asked, at times, to find a word that most closely matches the definition of the given word (find the synonym of the given word). You might also be asked for find the word that is closest to the opposite of a given word (find the antonym of a given word). It would pay to, as you learn new words and look them up in the dictionary, closely look at any synonyms or antonyms that are listed by the definition. Online dictionaries usually list them. Print dictionaries do sometimes, but your mileage may vary depending on your specific dictionary.

Test Your Knowledge: Vocabulary

For the following questions, select the answer choice with the word or words that best fit in the sentence.

1. The investor seemed almost_____: she knew which stocks to select before they rose in value.
    a. Circumspect
    b. Prescient
    c. Audacious
    d. Discerning
    e. Obtuse

2. The team of biologists was well prepared for the _____ climate in which they would be working; the tents and clothing they brought were all _____ to water.
    a. Equatorial…Impervious
    b. Arid…Impenetrable
    c. Humid…Porous
    d. Parched…Repulsive
    e. Tempestuous…Susceptible

3. Library cataloguing systems have always been important in _____ vast collections of knowledge; however, as information is increasingly_____, methods of organizing it are changing.
    a. Organizing…Diminished
    b. Documenting…Depleted
    c. Confounding…Uploaded
    d. Systematizing…Digitized
    e. Collating…Proliferated

4. Linda went to the meeting on the _____ of hearing about the new plan; in reality, she went because she wanted to spend some time away from her desk.
    a. Hunch
    b. Rationale
    c. Pretext
    d. Motive
    e. Deception

5. If elected, the candidate's first priority would be to ____ the laws which were negatively affecting his constituency.
    a. Allay
    b. Sanction
    c. Abrogate
    d. Ratify
    e. Lampoon

6. The chefs disagreed about the effect of an unusual spice in the dish; one felt that it added ____ to an otherwise standard meal, while the other maintained that it _ the cuisine.
    a. Pungency…Ravaged
    b. Relish…Augmented
    c. Redolence…Buttressed
    d. Drivel…Rectified
    e. Zest…Undermined

7. It is important to think _____ when learning about a new place because the culture, history, geography, and politics all interact to enable true understanding.
    a. Discordantly
    b. Discretely
    c. Critically
    d. Holistically
    e. Authentically

8. Astronomers in the 15th century were not using the types of _____ instruments we have today; rather, they successfully_____ the distances between planetary bodies using observations and what they understood about physics on Earth.
    a. Precise…Deduced
    b. Redundant…Concluded
    c. Meticulous…Appraised
    d. Efficacious…Promulgated
    e. Sophisticated…Generalized

9. In order to_____ the tradition, the family members made an effort to _____ the younger generation in the way that they had done it in the past.
    a. Nullify…Assuage
    b. Extend…Indoctrinate
    c. Formalize…Assimilate
    d. Deemphasize…Edify
    e. Perpetuate…Instruct

10. The play had a(n) _____ tone; all the patrons left the theater chortling and pleased.
    a. Ecstatic
    b. Jovial
    c. Somber
    d. Analytic
    e. Melancholy

11. Jeff was absolutely _____ about his idea; try as we might, we could not dissuade him.
   a. Parsimonious
   b. Relenting
   c. Adamant
   d. Pragmatic
   e. Capricious

12. In weaving cloth with threads, one draws the weft, or horizontal yarns, through the warp yarns, or the vertical, in an even and _____ manner to create a tight cloth.
   a. Consistent
   b. Oblique
   c. Imaginative
   d. Wholesome
   e. Substantial

13. College students quickly learn that _____ can be much more valuable than _____; all the intelligence in the world does not help if you are not able to manage your time.
   a. Perspicacity…Ambition
   b. Decorum…Alacrity
   c. Efficiency…Aptitude
   d. Accountability…Solicitude
   e. Wiliness…Acumen

14. Clarissa was grateful for her friend's assistance with editing down her originally _____ acceptance speech.
   a. Turgid
   b. Mellifluous
   c. Dilated
   d. Laconic
   e. Concise

15. "The party was an unmitigated disaster," Josephine said with _____, unworried about hurting anyone's feelings.
   a. Barbarity
   b. Vexation
   c. Elation
   d. Ire
   e. Candor

16. The Natural History Museum had an extensive exhibit which explained how scientists were able to learn the habits of _____ mammals from the _____ remains of their bodies.
    a. Extinct…Ossified
    b. Reserved…Mummified
    c. Omnivorous…Decayed
    d. Ambiguous…Coded
    e. Wary…Petrified

17. Erin _____ the volume of the music coming through her headphones in an effort to _____ the conversation of the men sitting behind her on the bus.
    a. Diminished…Conceal
    b. Terminated…Transcribe
    c. Maximized…Amplify
    d. Elevated…Obstruct
    e. Mitigated…Fathom

18. It is our opinion that preventing others from accessing information that could be helpful to them is _____ act.
    a. A transient
    b. An exceptionable
    c. A tractable
    d. An irascible
    e. An egalitarian

19. We _____ rejected the amendment; no argument or plea could persuade us to reverse our position.
    a. Equivocally
    b. Harmoniously
    c. Lugubriously
    d. Categorically
    e. Ambiguously

20. Even though the latest tests had _____ an outbreak as a possibility, the _____ of the epidemic continued to frighten the research team.
    a. Eliminated…Ruse
    b. Fourished…Reprieve
    c. Eradicated…Specter
    d. Delineated…Chance
    e. Subjugated…Theory

21. The author was rarely intrigued by the _____ details of detective work; rather, he explored the exciting moments of danger and suspense.
    a. Mundane
    b. Anxious
    c. Listless
    d. Copious
    e. Definitive

22. The introduction to the new edition of essays _____ the virtues of the author, who had won several literary prizes.
    a. Impugned
    b. Extolled
    c. Revamped
    d. Improvised
    e. Desecrated

23. Given the limited resources available, it would not be _____ to _____ what we have.
    a. Boorish…Appropriate
    b. Asinine…Aggregate
    c. Expedient…Squander
    d. Prudent…Inhibit
    e. Facetious…Ruin

24. The fundraising dinner at the museum was attended by a _____ group of artists, business owners, students, socialites, and publishers.
    a. Heterogeneous
    b. Contentious
    c. stimulating
    d. Prosaic
    e. Outlandish

25. Niku refused to acknowledge the _____ in her opinion against the expansion of tourism while she herself invested in the _____ chain of hotels.
    a. Duplicity…Extravagant
    b. Consistency…Growing
    c. Righteousness…Declining
    d. Hypocrisy…Burgeoning
    e. Relevance…Lucrative

26. What does **gouge** mean?
    a. decorate without taste
    b. completely enclose
    c. make a groove in
    d. convert text to computer code

27. Which of the following is closest to the term **refractory**?
- a. a grandmother who is sympathetic
- b. a defiant teenager
- c. a charismatic business man
- d. a dedicated police officer

28. Which of the following words most closely matches the definition of **supersede**?
- a. gain superpowers
- b. replace
- c. scare
- d. undulate

29. What does **stolid** mean?
- a. being down in the dumps
- b. showing excitement
- c. characterized by high humidity
- d. revealing very little sensibility or emotion

30. What does **placate** mean?
- a. destroy
- b. appease
- c. make worse
- d. hard

31. Inadvertently means:
- a. accidentally
- b. with contempt
- c. did alone
- d. immediately

32. "The informant **apprised** the officer of the situation." What does **apprised** mean in this context?
- a. told negatively
- b. provided with food
- c. got rid of
- d. made aware of

33. What does **efficacy** mean?
- a. having legal ability
- b. being judicious
- c. the power to cause a desired effect
- d. tolerance

34. What is an antonym of **diffidence**?
- a. confidence
- b. alarm
- c. aversion
- d. longing

35. What is the definition of **tractable**?
- a. reacting to suggestions quickly
- b. unhealthy
- c. softly
- d. in a strong way

36. Lethargic means:
- a. not reciprocated
- b. lacking activity or alertness
- c. having good fortune
- d. alone

37. The closest word to the definition of **pragmatic** is:
- a. precocious
- b. lonely
- c. practical
- d. conductive

38. To be deliberately ambiguous or unclear is to:
- a. equalize
- b. compare
- c. dress well
- d. equivocate

39. To be mixed with impurities is to be:
- a. seamless
- b. wasteful
- c. adulterated
- d. dirty

40. To **discredit** is to:
- a. predict
- b. reject as false
- c. make warm
- d. alert

Test Your Knowledge: Vocabulary – Answers

1. **b)**
   Prescient: Having knowledge of things or events before they happen; having foresight.

2. **a)**
   Equatorial: Typical of the regions at the earth's equator. **Impervious**: Not permitting penetration or passage.

3. **d)**
   Systematizing: Making systematic; arranging in a system. **Digitized**: Converting to digital form.

4. **c)**
   Pretext: Something put forward to conceal a true purpose.

5. **c)**
   Abrogate: To abolish by formal or official means.

6. **e)**
   Zest: An agreeable flavor imparted to something. **Undermined**: To injure or destroy something by stages.

7. **e)**
   Holistically: Incorporating the principle that whole entities have an existence greater than the sum of their parts.

8. **a)**
   Precise: Operating with total accuracy. **Deduced**: Arrived at a conclusion from something known; to infer.

9. **e)**
   Perpetuate: To preserve from extinction. **Instruct**: To furnish with knowledge.

10. **b)**
    Jovial: Characterized by a hearty, joyous humor.

11. **b)**
    Adamant: Utterly unyielding in attitude or opinion despite all appeals.

12. **a)**
    Consistent: Steady; even.

13. **b)**
    Efficiency: The production of desired effects with minimum waste of time or effort. **Aptitude**: Inherent ability; intelligence.

14. **a)**

   Turgid: Swollen; pompous.

15. **e)**

   Candor: Openness; honesty.

16. **a)**

   Extinct: No longer in existence. Ossified: the calcification of soft tissue into bonelike material.

17. **d)**

   Elevated: Raised. Obstruct: block out.

18. **b)**

   Exceptionable: Objectionable.

19. **d)**

   Categorically: Without exceptions or conditions; absolute.

20. **c)**

   Eradicated: Removed or destroyed utterly. **Specter**: Some object or source of terror or dread.

21. **a)**

   Mundane: Common; ordinary; banal.

22. **b)**

   Extolled: Praised lavishly.

23. **c)**

   Expedient: Suitable or wise under the circumstance. **Squander**: Use wastefully.

24. **a)**

   Heterogeneous: Different in kind, unlike; incongruous.

25. **d)**

   Hypocrisy: Pretense of morality that one does not really possess. **Burgeoning**: Growing or developing quickly.

26. **c)**

27. **b)**

28. **b)**

29. **d)**

30. **b)**

31. **a)**

32. **d)**

33. **c)**

34. **a)**

35. **a)**

36. **b)**

37. **c)**

38. **d)**

39. **c)**

40. **b)**

Chapter 3: Language – Multiple Choice

The multiple-choice writing questions include sentence improvement questions and error identification questions, both of which require an understanding of correct grammar and usage.

The following is a sample of the kind of sentence improvement questions you will encounter on the CHSPE. Carefully read and answer these questions, and then check your answers afterwards.

Paragraph A
(1) Of the two types of eclipses, the most common is the lunar eclipse, which occurs when a full moon passes through Earth's shadow. (2) The disc-shaped moon slowly disappears completely or turns a coppery red color. (3) Solar and lunar eclipses both occur from time to time.

Paragraph B
(4) During a solar eclipse, the moon passes between the Earth and Sun. (5) As the moon moves into alignment, it blocks the light from the Sun creating an eerie darkness. (6) When the moon is perfectly in position, the Sun's light is visible as a ring, or corona, around the dark disc of the moon. (7) A lunar eclipse can be viewed from anywhere on the nighttime half of Earth, a solar eclipse can only be viewed from a zone that is only about 200 miles wide and covers about one-half of a percent of Earth's total area.

1. Sentence 1: "Of the two types of eclipses, the most common is the lunar eclipse, which occurs when a full moon passes through Earth's shadow." What revision is necessary in this sentence?
    a) Change "most" to "more."
    b) Change "occurs" to "occur."
    c) Change "which" to "that."
    d) Change "Earth's" to "Earths'."
    e) No correction is necessary.

2. Sentence 2: "The disc-shaped moon slowly disappears completely or turns a coppery red color." If you rewrote sentence 2, beginning with "The disc-shaped moon slowly turns a coppery red color," the next word should be:
    a) And.
    b) But.
    c) When.
    d) Because.
    e) Or.

3. Paragraph A's effectiveness could be improved by making which revision?

    a) No revision is necessary.

    b) Move sentence 3 to the beginning of the paragraph.

    c) Remove sentence 2.

    d) Move sentence 2 to the beginning of the paragraph.

    e) Remove sentence 1.

4. Sentence 7: "A lunar eclipse can be viewed from anywhere on the nighttime half of <u>Earth, a solar eclipse</u> can only be viewed from a zone that is only about 200 miles wide and covers about one-half of a percent of Earth's total area." Select the option that indicates the best way to rewrite the underlined part of this sentence. If the original is the best way, choose option **a)**.

    a) "Earth, a solar eclipse"

    b) "Earth a solar eclipse"

    c) "Earth; a solar eclipse"

    d) "Earth, because a solar eclipse"

    e) "Earth, when a solar eclipse"

Answers:

1. a)

Use the comparative "more" when comparing only two things. Here, you comparing two types of eclipses, so "more" is correct. The other changes introduce errors.

2. e)

The clauses are joined by the conjunction "or" in the original sentence. Maintaining this conjunction maintains the original relationship between ideas.

3. b)

As sentence 3 would serve as a good topic sentence, as well as an effective lead into sentence 1, the paragraph could be improved by moving sentence 3 to the beginning.

4. c)

The two related sentences should be separated by a semicolon. The other answers introduce incorrect punctuation or an inaccurate relationship between the sentences.

BASIC REVIEW: LANGUAGE

The following pages will refresh your knowledge of basic grammatical structures, of which you must have a firm command for both the multiple choice and essay portion of the Language Section. Also review those concepts explained in the Reading Comprehension and Vocabulary Chapters of this book – particularly that of diction, word choice, and topic sentences; all will help in expanding and refining your language skills.

Nouns, Pronouns, Verbs, Adjectives, and Adverbs

Nouns

Nouns are people, places, or things. They are typically the subject of a sentence. For example, "The hospital was very clean." The noun is "hospital;" it is the "place."

Pronouns

Pronouns essentially "replace" nouns. This allows a sentence to not sound repetitive. Take the sentence: "Sam stayed home from school because Sam was not feeling well." The word "Sam" appears twice in the same sentence. Instead, you can use a pronoun and say, "Sam stayed at home because *he* did not feel well." Sounds much better, right?

> **Most Common Pronouns:**
> - I, me, mine, my.
> - You, your, yours.
> - He, him, his.
> - She, her, hers.
> - It, its.
> - We, us, our, ours.
> - They, them, their, theirs.

Verbs

Remember the old commercial, "Verb: It's what you do"? That sums up verbs in a nutshell! Verbs are the "action" of a sentence; verbs "do" things.

They can, however, be quite tricky. Depending on the subject of a sentence, the tense of the word (past, present, future, etc.), and whether or not they are regular or irregular, verbs have many variations.

> **Example:** "He runs to second base." The verb is "runs." This is a "regular verb."

> **Example**: "I am 7 years old." The verb in this case is "am." This is an "irregular verb."

As mentioned, verbs must use the correct tense – and that tense must remain the same throughout the sentence. "I was baking cookies and eat some dough." That sounded strange, didn't it? That's because the two verbs "baking" and "eat" are presented in different tenses. "Was baking" occurred in the past; "eat," on the other hand, occurs in the present. Instead, it should be "**ate** some dough."

Adjectives

Adjectives are words that describe a noun and give more information. Take the sentence: "The boy hit the ball." If you want to know more about the noun "boy," then you could use an adjective to describe it. "The **little** boy hit the ball." An adjective simply provides more information about a noun or subject in a sentence.

Adverb

For some reason, many people have a difficult time with adverbs – but don't worry! They are really quite simple. Adverbs are similar to adjectives in that they provide more information; however, they describe verbs, adjectives, and even other adverbs. They do **not** describe nouns – that's an adjective's job.

Take the sentence: "The doctor said she hired a new employee."

It would give more information to say: "The doctor said she **recently** hired a new employee." Now we know more about *how* the action was executed. Adverbs typically describe when or how something has happened, how it looks, how it feels, etc.

Good vs. Well
A very common mistake that people make concerning adverbs is the misuse of the word "good."

"Good" is an adjective – things taste good, look good, and smell good. "Good" can even be a noun – "Superman does good" – when the word is speaking about "good" vs. "evil." HOWEVER, "good" is never an adverb.

People commonly say things like, "I did really good on that test," or, "I'm good." Ugh! This is NOT the correct way to speak! In those sentences, the word "good" is being used to describe an action: how a person **did**, or how a person **is**. Therefore, the adverb "well" should be used. "I did really **well** on that test." "I'm **well**."

The correct use of "well" and "good" can make or break a person's impression of your grammar – make sure to always speak correctly!

Test Your Knowledge: Multiple Choice

For questions 1 – 10, select the best segment to replace the underlined segment of the sentence.

1. Rod cells are found in the human <u>eye so they can absorb light to see in even dim environments</u>.
   a) "eye, but can absorb light to see in even dim environments."
   b) "eye to see in dim environments even by absorbing light."
   c) "eye and can absorb light to see in even dim environments."
   d) "eye and are absorbing light to see in even dim environments."
   e) "eye so they can absorb light to see in even dim environments."

2. Having already finished her essay, <u>washing the truck was the thing Maricela was ready to do</u>.
   a) "washing the truck was the next thing Maricela did."
   b) "Maricela had another thing she was ready to do and that was washing the truck."
   c) "washing the truck Maricela was ready to do."
   d) "Maricela was ready to wash the truck."
   e) "washing the truck was the thing Maricela was ready to do."

3. The information gathered from the national census <u>is used to determine political boundaries, inform policies, and planning transportation systems</u>.
   a) "is used to determine political boundaries, inform policies, and plan transportation systems."
   b) "determines political boundaries and informs policies and plans transportation systems."
   c) "is determining political boundaries, informing policies, and planning transportation systems."
   d) "is used to determine political boundaries, informing policies, and planning transportation systems."
   e) "is used to determine political boundaries, inform policies, and planning transportation systems."

4. Many artists and producers disagree over how copyright laws <u>should be applied, they have different perspectives</u> on what best protects and encourages creativity.
   a) "should be applied since it is that they have different perspectives"
   b) "are applied with different perspectives"
   c) "should apply on differing perspectives"
   d) "are applied, because they have different perspectives"
   e) "should be applied, they have different perspectives"

5. Many consider television shows <u>to be eroding of our nation's imaginations and attention</u> <u>spans</u>.
    a) "to have eroded our nation's imaginations and attention spans."
    b) "erosion of our nation's imaginations and attention spans."
    c) "to be eroding of our national imaginations and attention spans."
    d) "to be eroding of the national imagination and attention span."
    e) "eroded our nation's imaginations and attention spans."

6. In the early 1960's, the Civil Rights movement in the United States <u>has swiftly grown to</u> <u>encompass</u> such movements as the Freedom Rides and the integration of universities.
    a) "has grown swiftly to encompass"
    b) "has swiftly grown, encompassing"
    c) "growing swiftly has encompassed"
    d) "had swiftly grown to encompass"
    e) "has swiftly grown to encompass"

7. Raul, the most knowledgeable of us all regarding physics, <u>maintain that we would be needing</u> better equipment.
    a) "maintaining that we would need"
    b) "maintains that we would be needing"
    c) "maintains that we would need"
    d) "maintain we would have needed"
    e) "maintain that we would be needing"

8. <u>Does anyone have an informed guess that they would like</u> to share before I reveal the answer?
    a) "Do anyone have an informed guess that they would like"
    b) "Is anyone having an informed guess that they would like"
    c) "Does anyone have an informed guess that they have wanting"
    d) "Anyone with an informed guess would like"
    e) "Does anyone have an informed guess that they would like"

9. <u>The meals at this restaurant have so much more salt in them than the restaurant we went to</u> <u>last week</u>.
    a) "The meals at this restaurant have so much more salt in them than that other restaurant."
    b) "The meals at this restaurant are so much saltier than the restaurant we went to last week."
    c) "The meals at this restaurant have much more salt in them than the restaurant we went to last week."
    d) "The meals at this restaurant have so much more salt in them than those at the restaurant we went to last week."
    e) "The meals at this restaurant have so much more salt in them than the restaurant we went to last week."

10. The Bernina Range <u>runs along eastern Switzerland and is considered to be a part of the</u> Central Eastern Alps.

    a) "is running along eastern Switzerland and is considered to be a part of the"

    b) "runs along eastern Switzerland and is considered part of"

    c) "run along eastern Switzerland, consider to be a part of the"

    d) "run along eastern Switzerland and is considered to be a part of the"

    e) "runs along eastern Switzerland and is considered to be a part of the"

For the following questions, select which of the underlined selections are incorrect within the sentence.

11. When cooking with hot <u>oil, it is prudent</u> for <u>one to wear</u> long sleeves so that want the oil does not <u>splatter onto</u> your arms and burn <u>them</u>.

    a) "oil, it is prudent"

    b) "one to wear"

    c) "splatter onto"

    d) "them."

    e) No error.

12. <u>Jordan and I</u> practiced our show <u>over and over;</u> we <u>would have</u> only twenty minutes to play, and we wanted to make sure <u>to play</u> our best songs.

    a) "Jordan and I"

    b) "over and over;"

    c) "would have"

    d) "to play"

    e) No error.

13. Aliyah asked <u>Timothy and I</u> to help her run the student <u>election;</u> so this week <u>we are hanging</u> posters, printing the ballots, <u>and editing speeches</u>.

    a) "Timothy and I"

    b) "election"

    c) "we are hanging"

    d) "and editing speeches."

    e) No error.

14. The difficulty with navigating <u>subway systems</u> <u>are compounded</u> <u>when some</u> stations are closed for <u>repair</u>.

    a) "subway systems"

    b) "are compounded"

    c) "when some"

    d) "repair."

    e) No error.

15. We <u>were given</u> explicit instructions for how to deal with <u>this exact</u> situation: we are to <u>immediately halt</u> production <u>and be contacting</u> the supervisor.
    a) "were given"
    b) "this exact"
    c) "to immediately halt"
    d) "and be contacting"
    e) No error.

16. The way the <u>shadows play</u> across the leaves <u>provide the artist</u> with <u>innumerable</u> challenges in painting the <u>twilit landscape</u>.
    a) "shadows play"
    b) "provide the artist"
    c) "innumerable"
    d) "the twilit landscape"
    e) No error.

17. <u>Along the banks</u> of the Colorado River <u>grow many different kinds</u> of bushes and trees <u>which serve</u> as habitats for the deer mice, raccoons, jackrabbits, and toads <u>that live there</u>.
    a) "Along the banks"
    b) "grow many different kinds"
    c) "which serve"
    d) "that live there"
    e) No error.

18. Gerald <u>slung his arm</u> about me <u>very</u> <u>familiar, although</u> we had <u>only met hours ago</u>.
    a) "slung his arm"
    b) "very"
    c) "familiar, although"
    d) "only met hours ago"
    e) No error.

19. After hiking <u>all afternoon</u> in the rocky desert, <u>we had</u> a desperate <u>need of</u> water bottles and <u>long, soothing showers</u>.
    a) "all afternoon"
    b) "we had"
    c) "need of"
    d) "long, soothing showers"
    e) No error.

20. It took nearly <u>half an hour</u> to dish out the meals to the large group. First, we had to <u>give everyone food</u>, and then we had to make sure <u>that everyone got</u> <u>their beverage</u> as well.

    a) "half an hour"
    b) "give everyone food"
    c) "that everyone got"
    d) "their beverage"
    e) No error.

21. When considering <u>what kind of</u> car to purchase, it is important to <u>factor in hidden costs</u> such as how much gas <u>the car consumed</u> and how expensive <u>maintenance will be</u>.

    a) "what kind of"
    b) factor in hidden costs"
    c) "the car consumed
    d) "maintenance will be"
    e) No error.

22. Just before <u>the guests arrived</u> Sarah realized that <u>we were going</u> to run out of paper plates, so <u>her and David</u> went to the store to buy <u>some</u>.

    a) "the guests arrived"
    b) "we were going"
    c) "her and David"
    d) "some"
    e) No error.

23. <u>Regardless by</u> how much one <u>likes or appreciates</u> a gift, it is <u>absolutely necessary</u> to thank the giver in person, by telephone, <u>or even with</u> a card.

    a) "Regardless by"
    b) "likes or appreciates"
    c) "absolutely necessary"
    d) "or even with"
    e) No error.

24. Even though Alaina <u>was generally cautious</u> when it came to daring physical feats, she was excited <u>to try</u> spelunking for the first time; <u>she'd heard</u> that <u>the caves were</u> breathtaking.

    a) "was generally cautious"
    b) "to try"
    c) "she'd heard"
    d) "the caves were"
    e) No error.

25. The <u>borders of</u> Rasco County <u>is comprised</u> of the river to the north <u>and east</u> and interstates <u>along the south</u> and the west.
    a) "borders of"
    b) "is comprised"
    c) "and east"
    d) "along the south"
    e) No error.

26. Each <u>applicant for</u> the open time slot <u>was asked</u> to give <u>his opinion on</u> the best way to improve the radio <u>station's programming</u>.
    a) "applicant for"
    b) "was asked"
    c) "his opinion on"
    d) "station's programming"
    e) No error.

27. There <u>will likely never</u> be a general <u>consensus on</u> which <u>is best</u>: the sunrise <u>or</u> the sunset.
    a) "will likely never"
    b) "consensus on"
    c) "is best'
    d) "or"
    e) No error.

28. The storm drew <u>menacing</u> near the town <u>where</u> citizens <u>had been</u> warned to move down to <u>their</u> cellars.
    a) "menacing"
    b) "where"
    c) "had been"
    d) "their"
    e) No error.

29. There are some difficulties inherent <u>for moving</u> across the country. <u>One must</u> secure housing <u>remotely</u> and <u>transport</u> belongings great distances.
    a) "for moving"
    b) "One must"
    c) "remotely"
    d) "transport"
    e) No error.

30. <u>When driving</u> on a <u>major</u> road, <u>to have gone</u> the speed limit <u>is prudent</u>.
    a) "When driving"
    b) "major"
    c) "to have gone"
    d) "is prudent"
    e) No error.

31. Salvador <u>and me</u>, <u>who take</u> Spanish class <u>together</u>, often study in the library <u>prior to</u> exams.

    a) "and me"
    b) "who take"
    c) "together"
    d) "prior to"
    e) No error.

32. <u>Because of</u> the stringent law <u>enacted in</u> the state, legislators <u>must be careful</u> to review <u>policies</u>.

    a) "Because of"
    b) "enacted in"
    c) "must be careful"
    d) "policies"
    e) No error.

33. <u>If the candidate</u> the company <u>had endorsed</u> were <u>to win</u>, the CEO <u>is very</u> pleased.

    a) "If the candidate"
    b) "had endorsed"
    c) "to win"
    d) "is very"
    e) No error.

34. <u>Even though</u> we <u>already understood</u> the solution, the tutor <u>insisted on</u> explaining the steps again to Sara <u>and I</u>.

    a) "Even though"
    b) "already understood"
    c) "insisted on"
    d) "and I"
    e) No error.

35. It is essential to <u>applying</u> the <u>criteria</u> uniformly across all of the candidates <u>in order to</u> judge the contest <u>fairly</u>.

    a) "applying"
    b) "criteria"
    c) "in order to"
    d) "fairly"
    e) No error.

For the following questions, rewrite the sentence in your mind using the provided start of the sentence, then choose the correct answer for what should follow.

36. Ice, which expands when frozen, will take up more space within the container holding it.

Rewrite, beginning with: <u>Expanding when frozen,</u>

The next words will be:

a) "the container holding it"
b) "take up more space"
c) "space is taken"
d) "ice will take up"
e) "holding it"

37. Michael, John, and Jerry all enjoy playing football on warm summer mornings if they can find a team to join them.

Rewrite, beginning with: <u>On warm summer mornings,</u>

The next words will be:

a) "Michael, John, and Jerry"
b) "playing football"
c) "enjoy the playing of"
d) "finding a team to join them"
e) "the team that joins them"

38. The office party was a success, everyone agreed happily, especially because of the good food.

Rewrite, beginning with: <u>Especially because of the good food,</u>

The next words will be:

a) "agreed"
b) "happily agreed"
c) "a success"
d) "the office"
e) "everyone agreed"

39. Dogs are faithful companions, and can be great addition to any family; but not all dogs are well-suited for hunting and outdoor activities.

Rewrite, beginning with: <u>A great addition to any family,</u>

The next words will be:

a) "All dogs"
b) "dogs are faithful"
c) "companions are"
d) "my dog is black"
e) "hunting and outdoor"

40. Jill was excited after finally learning how to ride a bike.

Rewrite, beginning with: <u>Finally learning how to ride a bike</u>

The next words will be:

    a) "was excited"
    b) "afterwards Jill"
    c) "she was riding"
    d) "excited Jill"
    e) "finally excited"

Test Your Knowledge: Multiple Choice – Answers

1. **c)**
   Wordiness and precision.

2. **d)**
   Misplaced modifier and wordiness.

3. **a)**
   Parallelism in listing, subject/verb agreement.

4. **d)**
   Word usage.

5. **a)**
   Verb tense.

6. **d)**
   Verb tense.

7. **c)**
   Subject/verb agreement and gerund use.

8. **e)**
   No error.

9. **d)**
   Imprecise comparisons.

10. **e)**
    No error.

11. **b)**
    "One" and "you" cannot both be used as forms of address in the same sentence.

12. **e)**
    No error.

13. **a)**
    Subject/object pronoun use ("Timothy and me").

14. **b)**
    Subject/verb agreement ("Difficulty is compounded")

15. **d)**
    Parallelism ("and contact")

16. **b)**

   Subject/verb agreement ("The way…provides the artist").

17. **e)**

   No error.

18. **c)**

   Adjective/adverb use ("familiarly although").

19. **c)**

   Proper idiomatic usage ("need for").

20. **d)**

   Subject/verb agreement ("everyone got his or her beverage").

21. **c)**

   Verb tense ("the car will consume").

22. **c)**

   Subject/object pronoun ("David and she went to the store").

23. **a)**

   Proper idiomatic usage ("Regardless of").

24. **e)**

   No error.

25. **b)**

   Subject/verb agreement ("are comprised").

26. **c)**

   Pronoun agreement ("his or her opinion").

27. **c)**

   Superlative use ("is better," since only two things are being compared).

28. **a)**

   Adjective/adverb use ("menacingly").

29. **a)**

   Idiomatic usage ("inherent in/to moving").

30. **c)**

   Verb tense ("going").

31. **a)**

Subject/object pronoun use ("and I").

32. **e)**

No error.

33. **d)**

Verb tense/subjunctive ("would be very").

34. **d)**

Subject/object pronoun use ("and me").

35. **a)**

Verb tense ("apply").

36. **d)**

37. **a)**

38. **e)**

39. **b)**

40. **d)**

Chapter 4: Language – Essay

Your essay will have the potential for a score of 1 to 5, with 5 being the highest.

- **Score of 4 – 5**: This is a well-written essay that addresses the topic clearly and coherently; is free of errors; has a well-supported argument that includes additional information; incorporates an easy-to-read format; and uses accurate word choice.

- **Score of 3**: This is an essay that might have a few minor errors in syntax or punctuation, but those do not detract from the readers' ability to understand the meaning. The essay presents a reasonably clear argument, although supporting arguments could have been better.

- **Score of 2**: This is an essay that initially addresses the topic, but quickly loses focus and confuses the reader. Word choice is poor, and the essay includes multiple errors which are distracting. Supporting arguments are very weak and do not relate well to the topic.

- **Score of 1**: An essay scoring a 1 generally does not address the topic at all, immediately losing focus and clarity. It contains serious errors which are not only distracting, but also cause confusion for the reader. These essays either have a lack of supporting arguments, or the supporting arguments are irrelevant to the topic.

An Effective Essay Demonstrates:

1. Insightful and effective development of a point-of-view on the issue.

2. Critical thinking skills. For example: Two oppositions are given; instead of siding with one, you provide examples in which both would be appropriate.

3. Organization. It is clearly focused and displays a smooth progression of ideas.

4. Supportive information. If a statement is made, it is followed by examples, reasons, or other supporting evidence.

5. Skillful use of varied, accurate, and apt vocabulary.

6. Sentence variety. (Not every sentence follows a "subject-verb" pattern. Mix it up!)

7. Proper grammar and spelling.

Things to Keep in Mind While Writing Your Essay

- **Rhetorical Force**: This factor judges how coherently the writer composes their essay. How clear is the idea or argument that is being presented?

- **Organization**: The writing must have a logical order, so that the reader can easily follow along and understand the main points being made.

- **Support and Development**: The use and quality of supporting arguments and information. Essays should not be vague.

- **Usage**: Essays should demonstrate a competent command of word choice, showing both accuracy and quality in the words used.

- **Structure and Convention**: Essays should be free of errors, including: spelling, punctuation, capitalization, sentence structure, etc.

- **Appropriateness**: Essays should be written in a style appropriate for the topic; they should also contain material appropriate for both the topic and the audience.

- **Timing**: You will only have about 30 – 35 minutes within which to write your essay. Pace yourself; and practice, practice, practice!

In this chapter, we will provide a sample CHSPE essay prompt, followed by four short sample responses. The four sample responses each display different qualities of work; an explanation will follow each sample, explaining what score it would have earned and why.

Essay Examples and Evaluations

Prompt:
Research tells us that what children learn in their earliest years is very important to their future success in school. Because of this, public schools all over the country are starting to offer Pre-Kindergarten classes.

What are the benefits of starting school early? What are some of the problems you see in sending four-year-olds to school?

Write a composition in which you weigh the pros and cons of public school education for Pre-Kindergartners. Give reasons and specific examples to support your opinion. There is no specific word limit for your composition, but it should be long enough to give a clear and complete presentation of your ideas.

Sample Score 4+ Essay

Today, more and more four-year-olds are joining their big brothers and sisters on the school bus and going to Pre-Kindergarten. Although the benefits of starting school early are clear, it is also clear that Pre-K is not for every child.

The students who are successful in Pre-K are ahead when they start kindergarten. Pre-K teaches them to play well with others. Even though it does not teach skills like reading and writing, it does help to prepare students for "real" school. Pre-K students sing songs, dance, paint and draw, climb and run. They learn to share and to follow directions. They tell stories and answer questions, and as they do, they add new words to their vocabularies. Pre-K can also give students experiences they might not get at home. They might take trips to the zoo or the farm, have visits from musicians or scientists, and so on. These experiences help the students better understand the world.

There are, however, some real differences among children of this age. Some four-year-olds are just not ready for the structure of school life. Some have a hard time leaving home, even for only three or four hours a day. Other children may already be getting a great preschool education at home or in daycare.

While you weigh the advantages and disadvantages of Pre-K, it is safe to say that each child is different. For some children, it is a wonderful introduction to the world of school. But others may not or should not be forced to attend Pre-K.

Evaluation of Sample Score 4 Essay

This paper is clearly organized and has stated a definite point of view. The paper opens with an introduction and closes with a conclusion. The introduction and conclusion combine an expression of the writer's opinion. Connections to the writer's opinion are made throughout the paper.

Sample Score 3 Essay

Just like everything in life, there are pros and cons to early childhood education. Pre-K classes work for many children, but they aren't for everyone. The plusses of Pre-K are obvious. Pre-K children learn many skills that will help them in kindergarten and later on. Probably the most important thing they learn is how to follow directions. This is a skill they will need at all stages of their life.

Other plusses include simple tasks like cutting, coloring in the lines, and learning capital letters. Many children don't get these skills at home. They need Pre-K to prepare them for kindergarten.

The minuses of Pre-K are not as obvious, but they are real. Children at this young age need the comfort of home. They need to spend time with parents, not strangers. They need that security. If parents are able to, they can give children the background they need to do well in school.

Other minuses include the fact that a lot of four year-old children can't handle school. They don't have the maturaty to sit still, pay attention, or share with others. Given another year, they may mature enough to do just fine in school. Sometimes it's better just to wait.

So there are definitely good things about Pre-K programs in our public schools, and I would definitely want to see one in our local schools. However, I think parents should decide whether their children are ready for a Pre-K education or not.

Evaluation of Sample Score 3 Essay

This paper has an identifiable organization plan, with pros and cons listed in order. The development is easy to understand, if not somewhat simplistic. The language of the paper is uneven, with some vague turns of phrase: "Just like everything in life," "definitely some good things." The word "maturity" is also misspelled. However, the essay is clear and controlled, and generally follows written conventions. If the writer had included more developed and explicit examples and used more varied words, this paper might have earned a higher score.

Sample Score 2 Essay

Is early childhood education a good idea? It depends on the child you're talking about. Some children probally need more education in the early years and need something to do to keep out of trouble. Like if there isnt any good nursry school or day care around it could be very good to have Pre-Kindergarten at the school so those children could have a good start on life. A lot of skills could be learned in Pre-Kindergarten, for example they could learn to write their name, cut paper, do art, etc.

Of course theres some kids who wouldnt do well, acting out and so on, so they might do better staying home than going to Pre-Kindergarten, because they just arent ready for school, and maybe wouldn't even be ready for kindergarten the next year either. Some kids just act younger than others or are too baby-ish for school.

So I would suport Pre-Kindergarten in our schools, it seems like a good idea to have someplace for those kids to go. Even if some kids wouldnt do well I think enough kids would do well, and it would make a diference in their grades as they got older. All those skills that they learned would help them in the future. If we did have Pre-Kindergarten it would help their working parents too, knowing their kids were someplace safe and learning importent things for life.

Evaluation of Sample Score 2 Essay

Although the writer of this paper has some good points to make, a lack of language skills, considerable misspellings, and a certain disconnectedness of thought keep the paper from scoring high. The paper begins with a vague introduction of the topic and ends with a paragraph that expresses the author's opinion, but the rest of the paper is disorganized. The reasons given do not always have examples to support them, and the examples that are given are weak.

Sample Score 1 Essay

What are benefits? What are some of problems with sending four-year-olds to school? Well, for one problem, its hard to see how little kids would do with all those big kids around at the school. They might get bullyed or lern bad habits, so I wouldnt want my four year old around those big kids on the bus and so on. Its hard to see how that could be good for a four year old. In our area we do have Pre-Kindergarten at our school but you dont have to go there a lot of kids in the program, I think about 50 or more, you see them a lot on the play ground mostly all you see them do is play around so its hard to see how that could be too usefull. They could play around at home just as easy. A reason for not doing Pre-Kindergarten is then what do you learn in Kindergarten. Why go do the same thing two years when you could just do one year when your a little bit bigger (older). I wonder do the people who want Pre-Kindergarten just want there kids out of the house or a baby sitter for there kids. Its hard to see why do we have to pay for that. I dont even know if Kindergarten is so usefull anyway, not like first grade where you actially learn something. So I would say theres lots of problems with Pre-Kindergarten.

Evaluation of Sample Score 1 Essay

This paper barely responds to the prompt. It gives reasons not to support Pre-K instruction, but it does not present any benefits of starting school early. The writer repeats certain phrases ("It's hard to see") to no real effect, and the faulty spelling, grammar, and punctuation significantly impede understanding. Several sentences wander off the topic entirely ("there a lot of kids in the program, I think about 50 or more, you see them a lot on the playground.", "I dont even know if Kindergarten is so usefull anyway, not like first grade where you actially learn something."). Instead of opening with an introduction, the writer simply lifts phrases from the prompt. The conclusion states the writer's opinion, but the reasons behind it are illogical and vague. Rather than organizing the essay in paragraph form, the writer has written a single, run-on paragraph. The lack of organization, weak language skills, and failure to address the prompt earn this essay a 1.

Test Your Knowledge: Essay

Prompt One

Provided below is an excerpt and a question. Use the excerpt to prompt your thinking, and then plan and write an essay in 35 minutes by answering the question from your perspective. Be sure to provide evidence.

- *General George S. Patton Jr. is quoted as having said, "No good decision was ever made in a swivel chair."*

Is it necessary to be directly in a situation in order to best understand what must be done?

Prompt Two

Provided below is an excerpt and a question. Use the excerpt to prompt your thinking, and then plan and write an essay in 35 minutes by answering the question from your perspective. Be sure to provide evidence.

- *In The Dispossessed, published in 1974, groundbreaking science fiction author Ursula K. LeGuin wrote, "You can't crush ideas by suppressing them. You can only crush them by ignoring them."*

Is it possible to get rid of an idea?

Prompt Three

Provided below is an excerpt and a question. Use the excerpt to prompt your thinking, and then plan and write an essay in 35 minutes by answering the question from your perspective. Be sure to provide evidence.

- *"The paradox of education is precisely this -- that as one begins to become conscious one begins to examine the society in which he is being educated." James Baldwin (1924-1987), American novelist, poet, and social critic*

Does a successful education require the examination of one's own society?

Test Your Knowledge: Essay – Answers

The following pages hold sample scored essays for topics one, two, and three. These are just examples - there are many ways that CHSPE essays can be scored high or low. Look for: reasoning, examples, word usage, coherency, and detail. There are no "right" answers on the CHSPE essay; the most important factor is that the argument be well developed.

Essays for Prompt One

Is it necessary to be directly in a situation to best understand what must be done?

Score of 4:

General George Patton was speaking of war when he noted that "no good decision was ever made in a swivel chair;" however, that observation applies to situations beyond battle. While a big-picture perspective is useful in analyzing situations and deciding how to act, an on-the-ground outlook is essential. In matters of politics, and technology, to name two, the best-laid plans usually have to be changed to respond to changing circumstances.

One example which illustrates the necessity of on-the-ground action is the famous space flight of Apollo 13. Before launch, all plans were worked out to get the manned mission to the moon and back. However, due to a fluke set of circumstances – an oxygen tank explosion and the resulting technical problems – the plans had to change. The successful return of Apollo 13 and the survival of its crew would not have been possible without the quick thinking of the men on board. They first noticed the incident, well before the technical crew in Houston would have detected it from Earth. While the work of the technical crew was of course key as well, without the astronauts on board the ship to implement an emergency plan, the mission would surely have been lost.

Just as there are often unforeseen circumstances when implementing technology, politics can also be unpredictable. For example, the Cuban Missile Crisis in 1962 required immediate, on-the-ground decision making by the leaders of the United States. Prior to the Cold War standoff, President Kennedy and his advisors had already decided their hardline position against Soviet weapons expansion in the Western hemisphere. The Monroe Doctrine, status quo since the 1920s, held that European countries should not practice their influence in the Americas. The Soviet Union tested this line by establishing intermediate-range missiles on the island of Cuba. President Kennedy could not simply hold to the established wisdom, because the true limits had never been tested. Instead, to stave off the threat of attack, he was forced to act immediately as events unfolded to preserve the safety of American lives. The crisis unfolded minute-by-minute, with formerly confident advisors unsure of the smartest step. Eventually, after thirteen tense days, the leaders were able to reach a peaceful conclusion.

What these events of the 1960s illustrate is that the best laid plans are often rendered useless by an unfolding situation. For crises to be resolved, whether they be in war, technology, or politics; leaders must have level heads in the moment with up-to-date information. Therefore, plans established in advance by those in swivel chairs with level heads are not always the best plans to follow. History has shown us that we must be able to think on our feet as unforeseen situations unfold.

Score of 3:

It is often necessary to be directly on the ground as a situation unfolds to know what is best do to. This is because situations can be unpredictable and what you previously thought was the best course of action, is not always so. This can be seen in the unfolding events of the 1962 Cuban Missile Crisis.

The Cuban Missile Crisis happened in 1962, during the presidency of John F. Kennedy, when Nikita Khrushchev, president of the Soviet Union, developed an intermediate-range missile base on the island of Cuba, within range of the United States. Since the Monroe Doctrine in the 1920s, the United States leaders have declared that they would not tolerate this kind of aggression. However, the decisions that had been made by leaders in the past, removed from the situation, were no longer relevant. It was necessary for President Kennedy to make decisions as events unfolded.

As the Cuban Missile Crisis shows us, at turning points in history decisions have to be made as events unfold by those who are in the middle of a situation. Otherwise, we would all be acting according to what those in the past and those removed from the challenge thought was best. Following the Monroe Doctrine could have resulted in unnecessary violence.

Score of 1 – 2:

It is necessary to make decisions while in the middle of a situation, not above the situation, because there is always information that is only known to people in the middle of the situation. For example, in a war, the strategists in Washington might have an overall aim in the war, but they would be unable to know what it best to do on the ground. Situations like running out of ammunition or the enemy having an unexpected backup could change the decisions that need to be made. This was especially true before cell phones and other digital technologies made communication easier.

Essays for Prompt Two

Is it possible to get rid of an idea?

Score of 4:

The suppression of ideas has been attempted over and over throughout history by different oppressive regimes. This theme has been explored as well in literature, through such dystopian works as 1984 and Fahrenheit 451. But these histories and stories always play out the same way: eventually, the repressed idea bubbles to the surface and triumphs. Ursula K. LeGuin acknowledged this by saying that ideas can be crushed not by suppression, but by omission.

In Aldous Huxley's novel <u>Brave New World</u>, the world government maintains order not by governing people strictly and policing their ideas, but by distracting them. Consumption is the highest value of the society. When an outsider to the society comes in and questions it, he is exiled – not to punish him, but to remove his influence from society. The government of the dystopia has learned that the best way to maintain control is to keep citizens unaware of other, outside ideas. This theme resonates with a modern audience more than other, more authoritarian tales of dystopia because in our society, we are less controlled than we are influenced and persuaded.

Repressing ideas through harsh authoritarian rule has proven time and again to be ultimately fruitless. For example, in Soviet Russia during the 1920s and 1930s, Josef Stalin attempted to purge his society of all religious belief. This was done through suppression: discriminatory laws were enacted, members of the clergy were executed, and the religious citizenry were terrified. While these measures drastically crippled religious institutions, they were ineffective at completely eliminating the idea of religion. Beliefs and traditions were passed down in communities clandestinely throughout the repressive rule of Stalin. After the fall of the Soviet Union, it became clear that religion had survived all along.

We see throughout literature and history that ignoring ideas and distracting people from them is generally more effective than to attempt to stamp an idea out through means of suppression. Authoritarian rule, in fact, can do the opposite: by dramatizing and calling attention to an idea in the name of condemning it, a regime might actually strengthen that idea.

Score of 3:

We have seen different governments try to crush out ideas throughout history. However, they are never actually successful in doing so. An idea can be ignored or suppressed, but it will never really go away. This is illustrated in the survival of religion in the Soviet Union.

In Soviet Russia during the 1920s and 1930s, Josef Stalin attempted to purge the society of all religious belief. This was done through suppression: discriminatory laws, execution of the clergy, and use of terror. While this harmed religious institutions, they were ineffective at crushing the idea of religion. Beliefs and traditions were passed down in communities secretly throughout the rule of Stalin. After the fall of the Soviet Union, it became clear that religion had survived all along.

The same kind of thing happened with apartheid law in South Africa. Even though there were laws against black Africans and white Africans using the same facilities, the idea caught fire, especially because of an international outcry against the law.

We see throughout history that suppressing ideas does not crush them. Authoritarian rule, in fact, can do the opposite: by calling attention to an idea in the name of condemning it, a regime might actually strengthen that idea.

Score of 1 – 2:

It is not possible to crush out an idea by ignoring it or by suppressing it. All throughout history, whenever anyone has tried to do this, they might be temporarily successful but the idea will always survive or come back. For example in the Soviet Union religion was suppressed. People were not allowed to practice their religion. But after the government fell, religion still existed – people had held on to their ideas during the time of suppression.

Essays for Prompt Three

Does a successful education require the examination of one's own society?

Score of 4:

James Baldwin noted that education is a paradox – as one becomes educated, one starts to question the educators. This is necessarily true, because an education is not just a mastery of facts and information but also acquiring the ability to think critically and forge new connections. Progress in society comes from people who understand the thought that came before and are then able to take it one step further. This theme plays out in social activism and in science, for example.

A society's understanding of human rights is constantly evolving. For this process to continue, each generation must question the mores taught by the previous generation. This process can be seen in America in the progression of women's rights, the rights of non-whites, religious rights, and the rights of the disabled. One hundred years ago, these groups had far less constitutional protection than they do today. It takes groups of educated people with a forward-thinking understanding to advocate and press for changes to be made. To take one example, women have gone from not having the right to vote in 1912 to, one hundred years later, women beginning to run for the highest political office. This happened because people like Elizabeth Cady Stanton, a suffragist in the 1850s, and Marsha Griffiths, the Representative in Congress in the 1970s who championed for the Equal Rights Amendment, were able to take the precepts of justice and equality taught to them and take them a step further by applying them to women's rights.

This pattern of taking knowledge a step further can also be seen in the fields of science and mathematics. Sir Isaac Newton, one of the inventors of calculus, is attributed with saying he "stood on the shoulders of giants." He took the concepts well established in mathematics – geometry and algebra – and used the tools in a new way to create calculus. To do this, he had to both already understand what was known in the field but also be able to look at it critically. Without people doing this, fields like science and math would never progress.

A society that is interested in advancing, in rights, science, and every other field, must educate its citizens not to only understand the knowledge of the past but also to criticize prior thought and look at things in a new way. This is what James Baldwin meant – a truly educated person will question everything, even his or her own society, in order to progress.

Score of 3:

James Baldwin noted that education is a paradox – as one becomes educated, one starts to question the educators. This is true because an education is not just a mastery of facts and information but also ability to think critically and forge new connections. Progress in society comes from people who understand the thought that came before and are then able to take it one step further. One example of this is in human and political rights.

A society's understanding of human rights is constantly evolving. For this process to continue, each generation must question the mores taught by the previous generation. This process can be seen in America in the progression of women's rights, the rights of non-whites, religious rights, and the rights of the disabled. One hundred years ago, these groups had far less constitutional protection than they do today. It takes groups of educated people with a forward-thinking understanding to press for changes to be made. To take one example, women have gone from not having the right to vote in 1912 to, one hundred years later, women beginning to run for the highest political office. This happened because people like Elizabeth Cady Stanton, a suffragist in the 1850s, and Marsha Griffiths, the Representative in Congress in the 1970s who championed for the Equal Rights Amendment, were able to take the precepts of justice and equality taught to them and take them a step further by applying them to women's rights.

A society that is interested in advancing, in rights every other field, must educate its citizens not to only understand the knowledge of the past but also to criticize prior thought and look at things in a new way. This is what James Baldwin meant – a truly educated person will question everything, even his or her own society, in order to progress.

Score of 1 – 2:

James Baldwin said that education is a paradox – as one becomes educated, one starts to question the educators. He is right about this, because being educated is not just about knowing the facts. It is also about critical thinking. Without thinking critically about one's own society, then people never make progress. This was necessary for things like civil rights, they could not just accept what was taught in the schools about the rights people should have. Probably the most important part of being educated is questioning the society you live in.

Chapter 5: Mathematics

The Most Common Mistakes

People make little mistakes all the time, but during a test those tiny mistakes can make the difference between a good score and a poor one. Watch out for these common mistakes that people make on the math section of the CHSPE:

- answering with the wrong sign (positive/negative)
- mixing up the order of operations
- misplacing a decimal
- not reading the question thoroughly (and therefore providing an answer that was not asked for)
- circling the wrong letter or filling in wrong circle choice

If you're thinking, *those ideas are just common sense*, that's exactly the point. Most of the mistakes made on the CHSPE are simple ones. But no matter how silly the mistake, a wrong answer still means a lost point on the test.

Strategies for the Mathematics Section

Go Back to the Basics

First and foremost, practice your basic skills: sign changes, order of operations, simplifying fractions, and equation manipulation. These are the skills used most on the CHSPE, though they are applied in different contexts. Remember that when it comes down to it, all math problems rely on the four basic skills of addition, subtraction, multiplication, and division. All you need to figure out is the order in which they're used to solve a problem.

Don't Rely on Mental Health

Using mental math is great for eliminating answer choices, but ALWAYS WRITE DOWN YOUR WORK! This cannot be stressed enough. Use whatever paper is provided; by writing and/or drawing out the problem, you are more likely to catch any mistakes. The act of writing things down also forces you to organize your calculations, leading to an improvement in your CHSPE score.

The Three-Times Rule

You should read each question at least three times to ensure you're using the correct information and answering the right question:
- **Step one:** Read the question and write out the given information.
- **Step two:** Read the question, set up your equation(s), and solve.
- **Step three:** Read the question and check that your answer makes sense (is the amount too large or small; is the answer in the correct unit of measure, etc.).

Make an Educated Guess

Eliminate those answer choices which you are relatively sure are incorrect, and then guess from the remaining choices. Educated guessing is critical to increasing your score.

Numbers and Operations

Positive and Negative Number Rules

Adding, multiplying, and dividing numbers can yield positive or negative values depending on the signs of the original numbers. Knowing these rules can help determine if your answer is correct.

$(+) + (−) =$ the sign of the larger number

$(−) + (−) =$ negative number

$(−) \times (−) =$ positive number

$(−) \times (+) =$ negative number

$(−) \div (−) =$ positive number

$(−) \div (+) =$ negative number

Examples

1. Find the product of −10 and 47.
    $$(−) \times (+) = (−)$$
    $$−10 \times 47 = \mathbf{−470}$$

2. What is the sum of −65 and −32?
    $$(−) + (−) = (−)$$
    $$−65 + −32 = \mathbf{−97}$$

3. Is the product of −7 and 4 less than −7, between −7 and 4, or greater than 4?
    $$(−) \times (+) = (−)$$
    $$−7 \times 4 = −28, \text{ which is } \textbf{less than } \mathbf{−7}$$

4. What is the value of −16 divided by 2.5?
    $$(−) \div (+) = (−)$$
    $$−16 \div 2.5 = \mathbf{−6.4}$$

Order of Operations

Operations in a mathematical expression are always performed in a specific order, which is described by the acronym PEMDAS:

1. Parentheses
2. Exponents

3. Multiplication

4. Division

5. Addition

6. Subtraction

Perform the operations within parentheses first, and then address any exponents. After those steps, perform all multiplication and division. These are carried out from left to right as they appear in the problem.

Finally, do all required addition and subtraction, also from left to right as each operation appears in the problem.

Examples

1. Solve: $[-(2)^2 - (4 + 7)]$

    First, complete operations within parentheses:
    $-(2)^2 - (11)$
    Second, calculate the value of exponential numbers:
    $-(4) - (11)$
    Finally, do addition and subtraction:
    $-4 - 11 = \mathbf{-15}$

2. Solve: $(5)^2 \div 5 + 4 \times 2$

    First, calculate the value of exponential numbers:
    $(25) \div 5 + 4 \times 2$
    Second, calculate division and multiplication from left to right:
    $5 + 8$
    Finally, do addition and subtraction:
    $5 + 8 = \mathbf{13}$

3. Solve the expression: $15 \times (4 + 8) - 3^3$

    First, complete operations within parentheses:
    $15 \times (12) - 3^3$
    Second, calculate the value of exponential numbers:
    $15 \times (12) - 27$
    Third, calculate division and multiplication from left to right:
    $180 - 27$
    Finally, do addition and subtraction from left to right:
    $180 - 27 = \mathbf{153}$

4. Solve the expression: $(\frac{5}{2} \times 4) + 23 - 4^2$

    First, complete operations within parentheses:
    $(10) + 23 - 4^2$

Second, calculate the value of exponential numbers:

$(10) + 23 - 16$

Finally, do addition and subtraction from left to right:

$(10) + 23 - 16$

$33 - 16 = \mathbf{17}$

Greatest Common Factor

The greatest common factor (GCF) of a set of numbers is the largest number that can evenly divide into all of the numbers in the set. To find the GCF of a set, find all of the factors of each number in the set. A factor is a whole number that can be multiplied by another whole number to result in the original number. For example, the number 10 has four factors: 1, 2, 5, and 10. (When listing the factors of a number, remember to include 1 and the number itself.) The largest number that is a factor for each number in the set is the GCF.

Examples

1. Find the greatest common factor of 24 and 18.

    Factors of 24: 1, 2, 3, 4, 6, 8, 12, 24

    Factors of 18: 1, 2, 3, 6, 9, 18

    The greatest common factor is 6.

2. Find the greatest common factor of 121 and 44.

    Since these numbers are larger, it's easier to start with the smaller number when listing factors.

    Factors of 44: 1, 2, 4, 11, 22, 44

    Now, it's not necessary to list all of the factors of 121. Instead, we can eliminate those factors of 44 which do not divide evenly into 121:

    121 is not evenly divisible by 2, 4, 22, or 44 because it is an odd number. This leaves only 1 and 11 as common factors, so the **GCF is 11**.

3. First aid kits are being assembled at a summer camp. A complete first aid kit requires bandages, sutures, and sterilizing swabs, and each of the kits must be identical to other kits. If the camp's total supplies include 52 bandages, 13 sutures, and 39 sterilizing swabs, how many complete first aid kits can be assembled without having any leftover materials?

    This problem is asking for the greatest common factor of 52, 13, and 39. The first step is to find all of the factors of the smallest number, 13.

Factors of 13: 1, 13

13 is a prime number, meaning that its only factors are 1 and itself. Next, we check to see if 13 is also a factor of 39 and 52:

$13 \times 2 = 26$

$13 \times 3 = 39$

$13 \times 4 = 52$

We can see that 39 and 52 are both multiples of 13. This means that **13 first aid kits can be made without having any leftover materials.**

4. Elena is making sundaes for her friends. She has 20 scoops of chocolate ice cream and 16 scoops of strawberry. If she wants to make identical sundaes and use all of her ice cream, how many sundaes can she make?

Arranging things into identical groups with no leftovers is always a tip that the problem calls for finding the greatest common factor. To find the GCF of 16 and 20, the first step is to factor both numbers:

Factors of 16: 1, 2, 4, 8, 16

Factors of 20: 1, 2, 4, 5, 10, 20

From these lists, we see that **4 is the GCF**. Elena can make 4 sundaes, each with 5 scoops of chocolate ice cream and 4 scoops of strawberry. Any other combination would result in leftover ice cream or sundaes that are not identical.

Comparison of Rational Numbers

Number comparison problems present numbers in different formats and ask which is larger or smaller, or whether the numbers are equivalent. The important step in solving these problems is to convert the numbers to the same format so that it is easier to see how they compare. If numbers are given in the same format, or after they have been converted, determine which number is smaller or if the numbers are equal. Remember that for negative numbers, higher numbers are actually smaller.

Examples

1. Is $4\frac{3}{4}$ greater than, equal to, or less than $\frac{18}{4}$?

These numbers are in different formats—one is a mixed fraction and the other is just a fraction. So, the first step is to convert the mixed fraction to a fraction:

$$4\frac{3}{4} = \frac{4 \times 4 + 3}{4} = \frac{19}{4}$$

Once the mixed number is converted, it is easier to see that $\frac{19}{4}$ is greater than $\frac{18}{4}$.

2. Which of the following numbers has the greatest value: 104.56, 104.5, or 104.6?

These numbers are already in the same format, so the decimal values just need to be compared. Remember that zeros can be added after the decimal without changing the value, so the three numbers can be rewritten as:

104.56

104.50

104.60

From this list, it is clearer to see that **104.60 is the greatest** because 0.60 is larger than 0.50 and 0.56.

3. Is 65% greater than, less than, or equal to $\frac{13}{20}$?

The first step is to convert the numbers into the same format. 65% is the same as $\frac{65}{100}$.

Next, the fractions need to be converted to have the same denominator. It is difficult to compare fractions with different denominators. Using a factor of $\frac{5}{5}$ on the second fraction will give common denominators:

$$\frac{13}{20} \times \frac{5}{5} = \frac{65}{100}$$

Now, it is easy to see that **the numbers are equivalent**.

Units of Measurement

You are expected to memorize some units of measurement. These are given below. When doing unit conversion problems (i.e., when converting one unit to another), find the conversion factor, then apply that factor to the given measurement to find the new units.

UNIT PREFIXES		
Prefix	**Symbol**	**Multiplication Factor**
tera	T	1,000,000,000,000
giga	G	1,000,000,000
mega	M	1,000,000
kilo	k	1,000
hecto	h	100
deca	da	10
base unit	--	--
deci	d	0.1
centi	c	0.01
milli	m	0.001
micro	μ	0.0000001
nano	n	0.0000000001
pico	p	0.0000000000001

UNITS AND CONVERSION FACTORS

Dimension	American	SI
length	inch/foot/yard/mile	meter
mass	ounce/pound/ton	gram
volume	cup/pint/quart/gallon	liter
force	pound-force	newton
pressure	pound-force per square inch	pascal
work and energy	cal/British thermal unit	joule
temperature	Fahrenheit	kelvin
charge	faraday	coulomb

Conversion Factors

1 in. = 2.54 cm	1 lb. = 0.454 kg
1 yd. = 0.914 m	1 cal = 4.19 J
1 mi. = 1.61 km	$1°F = \frac{5}{9}(°F - 32°C)$
1 gal. = 3.785 L	$1 cm^3 = 1 mL$
1 oz. = 28.35 g	1 hr = 3600 s

Examples

1.   A fence measures 15 ft. long. How many yards long is the fence?

   1 yd. = 3 ft.

   $\frac{15}{3}$ = **5 yd.**

2.   A pitcher can hold 24 cups. How many gallons can it hold?

   1 gal. = 16 cups

   $\frac{24}{16}$ = **1.5 gallons**

3. A spool of wire holds 144 in. of wire. If Mario has 3 spools, how many feet of wire does he have?

12 in. = 1 ft.

$\frac{144}{12}$ = 12 ft.

12 ft. × 3 spools = **36 ft. of wire**

4. A ball rolling across a table travels 6 inches per second. How many feet will it travel in 1 minute?

This problem can be worked in two steps: finding how many inches are covered in 1 minute, and then converting that value to feet. It can also be worked the opposite way, by finding how many feet it travels in 1 second and then converting that to feet traveled per minute. The first method is shown below.

1 min. = 60 sec.

(6 in.)/(sec.) × 60 s = 360 in.

1 ft. = 12 in.

(360 in.)/(12 in.) = **30 ft.**

5. How many millimeters are in 0.5 m?

1 meter = 1000 mm

0.5 meters = **500 mm**

6. A lead ball weighs 38 g. How many kilograms does it weigh?

1 kg = 1000 g

$\frac{38}{1000}$ g = **0.038 kg**

7. How many cubic centimeters are in 10 L?

1 L = 1000 ml

10 L = 1000 ml × 10

10 L = **10,000 ml or cm^3**

8. Jennifer's pencil was initially 10 centimeters long. After she sharpened it, it was 9.6 centimeters long. How many millimeters did she lose from her pencil by sharpening it?

$$1 \text{ cm} = 10 \text{ mm}$$

$$10 \text{ cm} - 9.6 \text{ cm} = 0.4 \text{ cm lost}$$

$$0.4 \text{ cm} = 10 \times .4 \text{ mm} = \textbf{4 mm were lost}$$

Decimals and Fractions

Adding and Subtracting Decimals

When adding and subtracting decimals, line up the numbers so that the decimals are aligned. You want to subtract the ones place from the ones place, the tenths place from the tenths place, etc.

Examples

1. Find the sum of 17.07 and 2.52.

    17.07

    +2.52

    19.59

2. Jeannette has 7.4 gallons of gas in her tank. After driving, she has 6.8 gallons. How many gallons of gas did she use?

    7.4

    − 6.8

    0.6 gal

Multiplying and Dividing Decimals

When multiplying decimals, start by multiplying the numbers normally. You can then determine the placement of the decimal point in the result by adding the number of digits after the decimal in each of the numbers you multiplied together.

When dividing decimals, you should move the decimal point in the divisor (the number you're dividing by) until it is a whole. You can then move the decimal in the dividend (the number you're dividing into) the same number of places in the same direction. Finally, divide the new numbers normally to get the correct answer.

Examples

1. What is the product of 0.25 and 1.4?

    $25 \times 14 = 350$

    There are 2 digits after the decimal in 0.25 and one digit after the decimal in 1.4.

    Therefore the product should have 3 digits after the decimal: **0.350** is the correct answer.

2. Find $0.8 \div 0.2$.

    Change 0.2 to 2 by moving the decimal one space to the right.

    Next, move the decimal one space to the right on the dividend. 0.8 becomes 8.

    Now, divide 8 by 2. $8 \div 2 = \mathbf{4}$

3. Find the quotient when 40 is divided by 0.25.

    First, change the divisor to a whole number: 0.25 becomes 25.

    Next, change the dividend to match the divisor by moving the decimal two spaces to the right, so 40 becomes 4000.

    Now divide: $4000 \div 25 = \mathbf{160}$

Working with Fractions

Fractions are made up of two parts: the **numerator**, which appears above the bar, and the **denominator**, which is below it. If a fraction is in its **simplest form**, the numerator and the denominator share no common factors. A fraction with a numerator larger than its denominator is an **improper fraction**; when the denominator is larger, it's a **proper fraction**.

Improper fractions can be converted into proper fractions by dividing the numerator by the denominator. The resulting whole number is placed to the left of the fraction, and the remainder becomes the new numerator; the denominator does not change. The new number is called a **mixed number** because it contains a whole number and a fraction. Mixed numbers can be turned into improper fractions through the reverse process: multiply the whole number by the denominator and add the numerator to get the new numerator.

Examples

1. Simplify the fraction $\frac{121}{77}$.

    121 and 77 share a common factor of 11. So, if we divide each by 11 we can simplify the fraction:

    $$\frac{121}{77} = \frac{11}{11} \times \frac{11}{7} = \frac{\mathbf{11}}{\mathbf{7}}$$

2. Convert $\frac{37}{5}$ into a proper fraction.

Start by dividing the numerator by the denominator:

$37 \div 5 = 7$ with a remainder of 2

Now build a mixed number with the whole number and the new numerator:

$$\frac{37}{5} = 7\frac{2}{5}$$

Multiplying and Dividing Fractions

To multiply fractions, convert any mixed numbers into improper fractions and multiply the numerators together and the denominators together. Reduce to lowest terms if needed.

To divide fractions, first convert any mixed fractions into single fractions. Then, invert the second fraction so that the denominator and numerator are switched. Finally, multiply the numerators together and the denominators together.

Examples

1. What is the product of $\frac{1}{12}$ and $\frac{6}{8}$?

Simply multiply the numerators together and the denominators together, then reduce:

$$\frac{1}{12} \times \frac{6}{8} = \frac{6}{96} = \frac{1}{16}$$

Sometimes it's easier to reduce fractions before multiplying if you can:

$$\frac{1}{12} \times \frac{6}{8} = \frac{1}{12} \times \frac{3}{4} = \frac{3}{48} = \frac{1}{16}$$

2. Find $\frac{7}{8} \div \frac{1}{4}$.

For a fraction division problem, invert the second fraction and then multiply and reduce:

$$\frac{7}{8} \div \frac{1}{4} = \frac{7}{8} \times \frac{4}{1} = \frac{28}{8} = \frac{7}{4}$$

3. What is the quotient of $\frac{2}{5} \div 1\frac{1}{5}$?

This is a fraction division problem, so the first step is to convert the mixed number to an improper fraction:

$$1\frac{1}{5} = \frac{5\times1+1}{5} = \frac{6}{5}$$

Now, divide the fractions. Remember to invert the second fraction, and then multiply normally:

$$\frac{2}{5} \div \frac{6}{5} = \frac{2}{5} \times \frac{5}{6} = \frac{10}{30} = \frac{1}{3}$$

4. A recipe calls for $\frac{1}{4}$ cup of sugar. If 8.5 batches of the recipe are needed, how many cups of sugar will be used?

This is a fraction multiplication problem: $\frac{1}{4} \times 8\frac{1}{2}$.

First, we need to convert the mixed number into a proper fraction:

$$8\frac{1}{2} = \frac{8 \times 2 + 1}{2} = \frac{17}{2}$$

Now, multiply the fractions across the numerators and denominators, and then reduce:

$$\frac{1}{4} \times 8\frac{1}{2} = \frac{1}{4} \times \frac{17}{2} = \frac{17}{8} \text{ cups of sugar}$$

Adding and Subtracting Fractions

Adding and subtracting fractions requires a **common denominator**. To find the common denominator, you can multiply each fraction by the number 1. With fractions, any number over itself (e.g., $\frac{5}{5}$, $\frac{12}{12}$, etc.) is equivalent to 1, so multiplying by such a fraction can change the denominator without changing the value of the fraction. Once the denominators are the same, the numerators can be added or subtracted.

To add mixed numbers, you can first add the whole numbers and then the fractions. To subtract mixed numbers, convert each number to an improper fraction, then subtract the numerators.

Examples

1. Simplify the expression $\frac{2}{3} - \frac{1}{5}$.

First, multiply each fraction by a factor of 1 to get a common denominator. How do you know which factor of 1 to use? Look at the other fraction and use the number found in that denominator:

$$\frac{2}{3} - \frac{1}{5} = \frac{2}{3}\left(\frac{5}{5}\right) - \frac{1}{5}\left(\frac{3}{3}\right) = \frac{10}{15} - \frac{3}{15}$$

Once the fractions have a common denominator, simply subtract the numerators:

$$\frac{10}{15} - \frac{3}{15} = \frac{7}{15}$$

2. Find $2\frac{1}{3} - \frac{3}{2}$.

This is a fraction subtraction problem with a mixed number, so the first step is to convert the mixed number to an improper fraction:

$$2\frac{1}{3} = \frac{2 \times 3 + 1}{3} = \frac{7}{3}$$

Next, convert each fraction so they share a common denominator:

$$\frac{7}{3} \times \frac{2}{2} = \frac{14}{6}$$

$$\frac{3}{2} \times \frac{3}{3} = \frac{9}{6}$$

Now, subtract the fractions by subtracting the numerators:

$$\frac{14}{6} - \frac{9}{6} = \frac{5}{6}$$

3. Find the sum of $\frac{9}{16}$, $\frac{1}{2}$, and $\frac{7}{4}$.

For this fraction addition problem, we need to find a common denominator.

Notice that 2 and 4 are both factors of 16, so 16 can be the common denominator:

$$\frac{1}{2} \times \frac{8}{8} = \frac{8}{16}$$

$$\frac{7}{4} \times \frac{4}{4} = \frac{28}{16}$$

$$\frac{9}{16} + \frac{8}{16} + \frac{28}{16} = \frac{45}{16}$$

4. Sabrina has $\frac{2}{3}$ of a can of red paint. Her friend Amos has $\frac{1}{6}$ of a can. How much red paint do they have combined?

To add fractions, make sure that they have a common denominator.

Since 3 is a factor of 6, 6 can be the common denominator:

$$\frac{2}{3} \times \frac{2}{2} = \frac{4}{6}$$

Now, add the numerators:

$$\frac{4}{6} + \frac{1}{6} = \frac{5}{6} \text{ of a can}$$

Converting Fractions to Decimals

Calculators are not allowed on the CHSPE V, which can make handling fractions and decimals intimidating for many test takers. However, there are several techniques you can use to help you convert between the two forms.

The first thing to do is simply memorize common decimals and their fractional equivalents; a list of these is given in Table 3.4. With these values, it's possible to convert more complicated fractions as well. For example, $\frac{2}{5}$ is just $\frac{1}{5}$ multiplied by 2, so $\frac{2}{5} = 0.2 \times 2 = 0.4$.

COMMON DECIMALS AND FRACTIONS	
fraction	decimal
$\frac{1}{2}$	0.5
$\frac{1}{3}$	$0.\overline{33}$
$\frac{1}{4}$	0.25
$\frac{1}{5}$	0.2
$\frac{1}{6}$	$0.1\overline{66}$
$\frac{1}{7}$	$0.\overline{142857}$
$\frac{1}{8}$	0.125
$\frac{1}{9}$	$0.\overline{11}$
$\frac{1}{10}$	0.1

Knowledge of common decimal equivalents to fractions can also help you estimate. This skill can be particularly helpful on multiple-choice tests like the CHSPE, where excluding incorrect answers can be just as helpful as knowing how to find the right one. For example, to find $\frac{5}{8}$ in decimal form for an answer, you can eliminate any answers less than 0.5 because $\frac{4}{8} = 0.5$. You may also know that $\frac{6}{8}$ is the same as $\frac{3}{4}$ or 0.75, so anything above 0.75 can be eliminated as well.

Another helpful trick can be used if the denominator is easily divisible by 100: in the fraction $\frac{9}{20}$, you know 20 goes into 100 five times, so you can multiply the top and bottom by 5 to get $\frac{45}{100}$ or 0.45.

If none of these techniques work, you'll need to find the decimal by dividing the denominator by the numerator using long division.

Examples

1.   Write $\frac{8}{18}$ as a decimal.

The first step here is to simplify the fraction:

$$\frac{8}{18} = \frac{4}{9}$$

Now it's clear that the fraction is a multiple of $\frac{1}{9}$, so you can easily find the decimal using a value you already know:

$$\frac{4}{9} = \frac{1}{9} \times 4 = 0.\overline{11} \times 4 = \mathbf{0.\overline{44}}$$

2. Write the fraction $\frac{3}{16}$ as a decimal.

None of the tricks above will work for this fraction, so you need to do long division:

The decimal will go in front of the answer, so now you know that $\frac{3}{16} = \mathbf{0.1875}$.

Converting Decimals to Fractions

Converting a decimal into a fraction is more straightforward than the reverse process is. To convert a decimal, simply use the numbers that come after the decimal as the numerator in the fraction. The denominator will be a power of 10 that matches the place value for the original decimal. For example, the numerator for 0.46 would be 100 because the last number is in the tenths place; likewise, the denominator for 0.657 would be 1000 because the last number is in the thousandths place. Once this fraction has been set up, all that's left is to simplify it.

Example

Convert 0.45 into a fraction.

The last number in the decimal is in the hundredths place, so we can easily set up a fraction:

$$0.45 = \frac{45}{100}$$

The next step is to simply reduce the fraction down to the lowest common denominator. Here, both 45 and 100 are divisible by 5: 45 divided by 5 is 9, and 100 divided by 5 is 20. Therefore, you're left with:

$$\frac{45}{100} = \frac{9}{20}$$

Ratios

A **ratio** tells you how many of one thing exists in relation to the number of another thing. Unlike fractions, ratios do not give a part relative to a whole; instead, they compare two values. For example, if you have 3 apples and 4 oranges, the ratio of apples to oranges is 3 to 4. Ratios can be written using words (3 to 4), fractions $\left(\frac{3}{4}\right)$, or colons (3:4).

In order to work with ratios, it's helpful to rewrite them as a fraction expressing a part to a whole. For example, in the example above you have 7 total pieces of fruit, so the fraction of your fruit that are apples is $\frac{3}{7}$, and oranges make up $\frac{4}{7}$ of your fruit collection.

One last important thing to consider when working with ratios is the units of the values being compared. On the CHSPE, you may be asked to rewrite a ratio using the same units on both sides. For example, you might have to rewrite the ratio 3 minutes to 7 seconds as 180 seconds to 7 seconds.

Examples

1. There are 90 voters in a room, and each is either a Democrat or a Republican. The ratio of Democrats to Republicans is 5:4. How many Republicans are there?

   We know that there are 5 Democrats for every 4 Republicans in the room, which means for every 9 people, 4 are Republicans.

   $5 + 4 = 9$

   Fraction of Democrats: $\frac{5}{9}$

   Fraction of Republicans: $\frac{4}{9}$

   If $\frac{4}{9}$ of the 90 voters are Republicans, then:

   $\frac{4}{9}$ x 90 = **40 voters are Republicans**

2. The ratio of students to teachers in a school is 15:1. If there are 38 teachers, how many students attend the school?

   To solve this ratio problem, we can simply multiply both sides of the ratio by the desired value to find the number of students that correspond to having 38 teachers:

   $\frac{15 \text{ students}}{1 \text{ teacher}} \times 38 \text{ teachers} = 570 \text{ students}$

   The school has **570 students**.

Proportions

A **proportion** is an equation which states that 2 ratios are equal. Proportions are usually written as 2 fractions joined by an equal sign $\left(\frac{a}{b} = \frac{c}{d}\right)$, but they can also be written using colons ($a : b :: c : d$). Note that in a proportion, the units must be the same in both numerators and in both denominators.

Often you will be given 3 of the values in a proportion and asked to find the 4th. In these types of problems, you can solve for the missing variable by cross-multiplying—multiply the numerator of each fraction by the denominator of the other to get an equation with no fractions as shown below. You can then solve the equation using basic algebra. (For more on solving basic equations, see *Algebraic Expressions and Equations*.)

$\frac{a}{b} = \frac{c}{d} \rightarrow ad = bc$

Examples

1. A train traveling 120 miles takes 3 hours to get to its destination. How long will it take for the train to travel 180 miles?

    Start by setting up the proportion:

    $$\frac{120 \text{ miles}}{3 \text{ hours}} = \frac{180 \text{ miles}}{x \text{ hours}}$$

    Note that it doesn't matter which value is placed in the numerator or denominator, as long as it is the same on both sides. Now, solve for the missing quantity through cross−multiplication:

    $120 \text{ miles} \times x \text{ hours} = 3 \text{ hours} \times 180 \text{ miles}$

    Now solve the equation:

    $$x = \frac{3 \text{ hours} \times 180 \text{ miles}}{120 \text{ miles}}$$

    $x = 4.5$ hours

2. One acre of wheat requires 500 gallons of water. How many acres can be watered with 2600 gallons?

    Set up the equation:

    $$\frac{1 \text{ acre}}{500 \text{ gal.}} = \frac{x \text{ acres}}{2600 \text{ gal.}}$$

    Then solve for x:

    $$x = \frac{1 \text{ acre} \times 2600 \text{ gal.}}{500 \text{ gal.}}$$

    $x = \frac{26}{5}$ or **5.2 acres**

3. If $35 : 5 :: 49 : x$, find x.

    This problem presents two equivalent ratios that can be set up in a fraction equation:

    $$\frac{35}{5} = \frac{49}{x}$$

    You can then cross-multiply to solve for x:

    $35x = 49 \times 5$

    $x = 7$

Percentages

A **percent** is the ratio of a part to the whole. Questions may give the part and the whole and ask for the percent, or give the percent and the whole and ask for the part, or give the part and the percent and ask for the value of the whole. The equation for percentages can be rearranged to solve for any of these:

$$percent = \frac{part}{whole}$$

$$part = whole \times percent$$

$$whole = \frac{part}{percent}$$

In the equations above, the percent should always be expressed as a decimal. In order to convert a decimal into a percentage value, simply multiply it by 100. So, if you've read 5 pages (the part) of a 10-page article (the whole), you've read $\frac{5}{10}$ = 0.5 or 50%. (The percent sign (%) is used once the decimal has been multiplied by 100.)

Note that when solving these problems, the units for the part and the whole should be the same. If you're reading a book, saying you've read 5 pages out of 15 chapters doesn't make any sense.

Examples

1. 45 is 15% of what number?

    Set up the appropriate equation and solve.

    Don't forget to change 15% to a decimal value:

    $$whole = \frac{part}{percent} = \frac{45}{0.15} = \textbf{300}$$

2. Jim spent 30% of his paycheck at the fair. He spent $15 for a hat, $30 for a shirt, and $20 playing games. How much was his check? (Round to nearest dollar.)

    Set up the appropriate equation and solve:

    $$whole = \frac{part}{percent} = \frac{15+30+20}{0.30} = \textbf{\$217.00}$$

3. What percent of 65 is 39?

    Set up the equation and solve:

    $$percent = \frac{part}{whole} = \frac{39}{65} = \textbf{0.6 or 60\%}$$

4. Greta and Max sell cable subscriptions. In a given month, Greta sells 45 subscriptions and Max sells 51. If 240 total subscriptions were sold in that month, what percent were not sold by Greta or Max?

    You can use the information in the question to figure out what percentage of subscriptions were sold by Max and Greta:

    $$percent = \frac{part}{whole} = \frac{51+45}{240} = \frac{96}{240} = 0.4 \text{ or } 40\%$$

    However, the question asks how many subscriptions weren't sold by Max or Greta. If they sold 40%, then the other salespeople sold 100% − 40% = **60%**.

5. Grant needs to score 75% on an exam. If the exam has 45 questions, at least how many does he need to answer correctly?

Set up the equation and solve. Remember to convert 75% to a decimal value:

$part = whole \times percent = 45 \times 0.75 = 33.75$, so he needs to answer at least **34 questions correctly**.

Percent Change

Percent change problems will ask you to calculate how much a given quantity changed. The problems are solved in a similar way to regular percent problems, except that instead of using the *part* you'll use the *amount of change*. Note that the sign of the *amount of change* is important: if the original amount has increased the change will be positive, and if it has decreased the change will be negative. Again, in the equations below the percent is a decimal value; you need to multiply by 100 to get the actual percentage.

$$percent\ change = \frac{amount\ of\ change}{original\ amount}$$

$$amount\ of\ change = original\ amount\ \times percent\ change$$

$$original\ amount = \frac{amount\ of\ change}{percent\ change}$$

Examples

1. A computer software retailer marks up its games by 40% above the wholesale price when it sells them to customers. Find the price of a game for a customer if the game costs the retailer $25.

Set up the appropriate equation and solve:

amount of change = original amount x *percent change* = $25 \times 0.4 = 10$

If the amount of change is 10, that means the store adds a markup of $10, so the game costs:

$25 + $10 = **$35**

2. A golf shop pays its wholesaler $40 for a certain club, and then sells it to a golfer for $75. What is the markup rate?

First, calculate the amount of change:

$75 - 40 = 35$

Now you can set up the equation and solve.

(Note that *markup rate* is another way of saying *percent change*):

$$percent\ change = \frac{amount\ of\ change}{original\ amount} = \frac{35}{40} = 0.875 = \textbf{87.5\%}$$

3. A store charges a 40% markup on the shoes it sells. How much did the store pay for a pair of shoes purchased by a customer for $63?

> You're solving for the original price, but it's going to be tricky because you don't know the amount of change; you only know the new price. To solve, you need to create an expression for the amount of change:
>
> If *original amount* = x
>
> Then *amount of change* = $63 - x$
>
> Now you can plug these values into your equation:
>
> $$original\ amount = \frac{amount\ of\ change}{percent\ change}$$
>
> $$x = \frac{63 - x}{0.4}$$
>
> The last step is to solve for x:
>
> $0.4x = 63 - x$
>
> $1.4x = 63$
>
> $x = 45$
>
> The store paid **$45 for the shoes**.

4. An item originally priced at $55 is marked 25% off. What is the sale price?

> You've been asked to find the sale price, which means you need to solve for the amount of change first:
>
> *amount of change = original amount × percent change* →
>
> $55 \times 0.25 = 13.75$
>
> Using this amount, you can find the new price. Because it's on sale, we know the item will cost less than the original price:
>
> $55 - 13.75 = 41.25$
>
> **The sale price is $41.25**.

5. James wants to put in an 18 foot by 51 foot garden in his backyard. If he does, it will reduce the size of this yard by 24%. What will be the area of the remaining yard?

> This problem is tricky because you need to figure out what each number in the problem stands for. 24% is obviously the percent change, but what about the measurements in feet? If you multiply these values you get the area of the garden (for more on area see *Area and Perimeter*):

$$18 \text{ ft.} \times 51 \text{ ft.} = 918 \text{ ft.}^2$$

This 918 ft.² is the amount of change—it's how much smaller the lawn is.

Now we can set up an equation:

$$original\ amount = \frac{amount\ of\ change}{percent\ change} = \frac{918}{0.24} = 3825$$

If the original lawn was 3825 ft.² and the garden is 918 ft.², then the remaining area is $3825 - 918 = 2907$.

The remaining lawn covers **2907 ft.²**

Probabilities

A **probability** is found by dividing the number of desired outcomes by the number of total possible outcomes. As with percentages, a probability is the ratio of a part to a whole, with the whole being the total number of things that could happen, and the part being the number of those things that would be considered a success. Probabilities can be written using percentages (40%), decimals (0.4), fractions $\left(\frac{2}{5}\right)$, or in words (probability is 2 in 5).

$$probability = \frac{desired\ outcomes}{total\ possible\ outcomes}$$

Examples

1.   A bag holds 3 blue marbles, 5 green marbles, and 7 red marbles. If you pick one marble from the bag, what is the probability it will be blue?

Because there are 15 marbles in the bag (3 + 5 + 7), the total number of possible outcomes is 15. Of those outcomes, 3 would be blue marbles, which is the desired outcome. With that information you can set up an equation:

$$probability = \frac{desired\ outcomes}{total\ possible\ outcomes} = \frac{3}{15} = \frac{1}{5}$$

The probability is **1 in 5 or 0.2 that a blue marble is picked.**

2.   A bag contains 75 balls. If the probability that a ball selected from the bag will be red is 0.6, how many red balls are in the bag?

Because you're solving for desired outcomes (the number of red balls), first you need to rearrange the equation:

$$probability = \frac{desired\ outcomes}{total\ possible\ outcomes} \rightarrow$$

$$desired\ outcomes = probability \times total\ possible\ outcomes$$

In this problem, the desired outcome is choosing a red ball, and the total possible outcomes are represented by the 75 total balls.

desired outcomes = $0.6 \times 75 = 45$

There are **45 red balls in the bag.**

3. A theater has 230 seats: 75 seats are in the orchestra area, 100 seats are in the mezzanine, and 55 seats are in the balcony. If a ticket is selected at random, what is the probability that it will be for either a mezzanine or balcony seat?

In this problem, the desired outcome is a seat in either the mezzanine or balcony area, and the total possible outcomes are represented by the 230 total seats, so the equation should be written as:

$$probability = \frac{desired\ outcomes}{total\ possible\ outcomes} = \frac{100+55}{230} = \mathbf{0.67}$$

4. The probability of selecting a student whose name begins with the letter *s* from a school attendance log is 7%. If there are 42 students whose names begin with *s* enrolled at the school, how many students attend the school?

Because you're solving for total possible outcomes (total number of students), first you need to rearrange the equation:

$$probability = \frac{desired\ outcomes}{total\ possible\ outcomes} \rightarrow$$

$$total\ possible\ outcomes = \frac{desired\ outcomes}{probability}$$

In this problem, you are given a probability (7% or 0.07) and the number of desired outcomes (42). These can be plugged into the equation to solve:

$$total\ possible\ outcomes = \frac{desired\ outcomes}{probability} = \frac{42}{0.07} = \mathbf{600}\ \textbf{students}$$

Algebra

Algebraic Expressions and Equations

Algebraic expressions and equations include a **variable**, which is a letter standing in for a number. These expressions and equations are made up of **terms**, which are groups of numbers and variables (e.g., $2xy$). An **expression** is simply a set of terms (e.g., $3x + 2xy$), while an **equation** includes an equal sign (e.g., $3x + 2xy = 17$). When simplifying expressions or solving algebraic equations, you'll need to use many different mathematical properties and operations, including addition, subtraction, multiplication, division, exponents, roots, distribution, and the order of operations.

Evaluating Algebraic Expressions

To evaluate an algebraic expression, simply plug the given value(s) in for the appropriate variable(s) in the expression.

Example

Evaluate $2x + 6y - 3z$ if , $x = 2$, $y = 4$, and $z = -3$.

Plug in each number for the correct variable and simplify:

$2x + 6y - 3z = 2(2) + 6(4) - 3(-3) = 4 + 24 + 9 =$ **37**

Adding and Subtracting Terms

Only like terms, which have the exact same variable(s), can be added or subtracted. Constants are numbers without variables attached, and those can be added and subtracted together as well. When simplifying an expression, like terms should be added or subtracted so that no individual group of variables occurs in more than one term. For example, the expression $5x + 6xy$ is in its simplest form, while $5x + 6xy - 11xy$ is not because the term xy appears more than once.

Example

Simplify the expression $5xy + 7y + 2yz + 11xy - 5yz$.

Start by grouping together like terms:

$(5xy + 11xy) + (2yz - 5yz) + 7y$

Now you can add together each set of like terms:

$16xy + 7y - 3yz$

Multiplying and Dividing Terms

To multiply a single term by another, simply multiply the coefficients and then multiply the variables. Remember that when multiplying variables with exponents, those exponents are added together. For example, $(x^5y)(x^3y^4) = x^8y^5$.

When multiplying a term by a set of terms inside parentheses, you need to **distribute** to each term inside the parentheses as shown below:

When variables occur in both the numerator and denominator of a fraction, they cancel each other out. So, a fraction with variables in its simplest form will not have the same variable on the top and bottom.

Examples

1.   Simplify the expression $(3x^4y^2z)(2y^4z^5)$.

        Multiply the coefficients and variables together:

        $3 \times 2 = 6$

        $y^2 \times y^4 = y^6$

        $z \times z^5 = z^6$

        Now put all the terms back together:

        $\boldsymbol{6x^4y^6z^6}$

2.   Simplify the expression: $(2y^2)(y^3 + 2xy^2z + 4z)$

        Multiply each term inside the parentheses by the term $2y^2$:

        $(2y^2)(y^3 + 2xy^2z + 4z)$

        $(2y^2 \times y^3) + (2y^2 \times 2xy^2z) \times (2y^2 \times 4z)$

        $\boldsymbol{2y^5 + 4xy^4z + 8y^2z}$

3.   Simplify the expression: $(5x + 2)(3x + 3)$

        Use the acronym FOIL—First, Outer, Inner, Last—to multiply the terms:

        First: $5x \times 3x = 15x^2$

        Outer: $5x \times 3 = 15x$

        Inner: $2 \times 3x = 6x$

        Last: $2 \times 3 = 6$

        Now combine like terms:

        $\boldsymbol{15x^2 + 21x + 6}$

4.   Simplify the expression: $\frac{2x^4y^3z}{8x^2z^3}$

        Simplify by looking at each variable and crossing out those that appear in the numerator and denominator:

        $\frac{2}{8} = \frac{1}{4}$

        $\frac{x^4}{x^2} = \frac{x^2}{1}$

        $\frac{z}{z^2} = \frac{1}{z}$

        $\frac{2x^4y^3z}{8x^2z^3} = \frac{x^2y^3}{4z}$

Solving Equations

To solve an equation, you need to manipulate the terms on each side to isolate the variable, meaning if you want to find x, you have to get the x alone on one side of the equal sign. To do this, you'll need to use many of the tools discussed above: you might need to distribute, divide, add, or subtract like terms, or find common denominators.

Think of each side of the equation as the two sides of a see-saw. As long as the two people on each end weigh the same amount the see-saw will be balanced: if you have a 120 lb. person on each end, the see-saw is balanced. Giving each of them a 10 lb. rock to hold changes the weight on each end, but the see-saw itself stays balanced. Equations work the same way: you can add, subtract, multiply, or divide whatever you want as long as you do the same thing to both sides.

Most equations you'll see on the CHSPE can be solved using the same basic steps:

1. Distribute to get rid of parentheses.

2. Use the least common denominator to get rid of fractions.

3. Add/subtract like terms on either side.

4. Add/subtract so that constants appear on only one side of the equation.

5. Multiply/divide to isolate the variable.

Examples

1. Solve for x: $25x + 12 = 62$

    This equation has no parentheses, fractions, or like terms on the same side, so you can start by subtracting 12 from both sides of the equation:

    $25x + 12 = 62$

    $(25x + 12) - 12 = 62 - 12$

    $25x = 50$

    Now, divide by 25 to isolate the variable:

    $\frac{25x}{25} = \frac{50}{25}$

    $x = 2$

2. Solve the following equation for x: $2x - 4(2x + 3) = 24$

    Start by distributing to get rid of the parentheses (don't forget to distribute the negative):

    $2x - 4(2x + 3) = 24 \rightarrow$

    $2x - 8x - 12 = 24$

There are no fractions, so now you can join like terms:

$2x - 8x - 12 = 24 \rightarrow$

$-6x - 12 = 24$

Now add 12 to both sides and divide by -6.

$-6x - 12 = 24$

$(-6x - 12) + 12 = 24 + 12 \rightarrow$

$-6x = 36 \rightarrow$

$\dfrac{-6x}{-6} = \dfrac{36}{-6}$

$x = -6$

3. Solve the following equation for x: $\dfrac{x}{3} + \dfrac{1}{2} = \dfrac{x}{6} - \dfrac{5}{12}$

Start by multiplying by the least common denominator to get rid of the fractions:

$\dfrac{x}{3} + \dfrac{1}{2} = \dfrac{x}{6} - \dfrac{5}{12} \rightarrow$

$12\left(\dfrac{x}{3} + \dfrac{1}{2}\right) = 12\left(\dfrac{x}{6} - \dfrac{5}{12}\right) \rightarrow$

$4x + 6 = 2x - 5$

Now you can isolate x:

$(4x + 6) - 6 = (2x - 5) - 6 \rightarrow$

$4x = 2x - 11 \rightarrow$

$(4x) - 2x = (2x - 11) - 2x \rightarrow$

$2x = -11 \rightarrow$

$x = \dfrac{11}{2}$

4. Find the value of x: $2(x + y) - 7x = 14x + 3$

This equation looks more difficult because it has 2 variables, but you can use the same steps to solve for x. First, distribute to get rid of the parentheses and combine like terms:

$2(x + y) - 7x = 14x + 3 \rightarrow$

$2x + 2y - 7x = 14x + 3 \rightarrow$

$-5x + 2y = 14x + 3$

Now you can move the x terms to one side and everything else to the other, and then divide to isolate x:

$-5x + 2y = 14x + 3 \rightarrow$

$-19x = -2y + 3 \rightarrow x = \dfrac{2y - 3}{19}$

Inequalities

Inequalities look like equations, except that instead of having an equal sign, they have one of the following symbols:

> Greater than: The expression left of the symbol is larger than the expression on the right.

< Less than: The expression left of the symbol is smaller than the expression on the right.

≥ Greater than or equal to: The expression left of the symbol is larger than or equal to the expression on the right.

≤ Less than or equal to: The expression left of the symbol is less than or equal to the expression on the right.

Inequalities are solved like linear and algebraic equations. The only difference is that the symbol must be reversed when both sides of the equation are multiplied by a negative number.

Example

Solve for x: $-7x + 2 < 6 - 5x$

Collect like terms on each side as you would for a regular equation:

$-7x + 2 < 6 - 5x \rightarrow$

$-2x < 4$

The direction of the sign switches when you divide by a negative number:

$-2x < 4 \rightarrow$

$x > -2$

Absolute Value

The **absolute value** of a number (represented by the symbol $|x|$) is its distance from zero, not its value. For example, $|3| = 3$, and $|-3| = 3$ because both 3 and -3 are three units from zero. The absolute value of a number is always positive.

Equations with absolute values will have two answers, so you need to set up two equations. The first is simply the equation with the absolute value symbol removed. For the second equation, isolate the absolute value on one side of the equation and multiply the other side of the equation by -1.

Examples

1. Solve for x: $|2x - 3| = x + 1$

> Set up the first equation by removing the absolute value symbol, then solve for x:
>
> $|2x - 3| = x + 1$
>
> $2x - 3 = x + 1$
>
> $x = 4$
>
> For the second equation, remove the absolute value and multiply by -1:
>
> $|2x - 3| = x + 1 \rightarrow$
>
> $2x - 3 = -(x + 1) \rightarrow$
>
> $2x - 3 = -x - 1 \rightarrow$
>
> $3x = 2$
>
> $x = 2/3$
>
> Both answers are correct, so the complete answer is $x = \mathbf{4}$ or $\dfrac{\mathbf{2}}{\mathbf{3}}$.

2. Solve for y: $2|y + 4| = 10$

> Set up the first equation:
>
> $2(y + 4) = 10 \rightarrow$
>
> $y + 4 = 5 \rightarrow$
>
> $y = 1$
>
> Set up the second equation. Remember to isolate the absolute value before multiplying by -1:
>
> $2|y + 4| = 10 \rightarrow$
>
> $|y + 4| = 5 \rightarrow$
>
> $y + 4 = -5$
>
> $y = -9$
>
> $y = \mathbf{1}$ or $\mathbf{-9}$

Statistics

Mean, Median, and Mode

Mean is a math term for average. To find the mean, total all the terms and divide by the number of terms. The **median** is the middle number of a given set. To find the median, put the terms in numerical order; the middle number will be the median. In the case of a set of even numbers, the middle two numbers are averaged. **Mode** is the number which occurs most frequently within a given set.

Examples

1. Find the mean of 24, 27, and 18.

   Add the terms, then divide by the number of terms:

   $$mean = \frac{24+27+18}{3} = 23$$

2. The mean of three numbers is 45. If two of the numbers are 38 and 43, what is the third number?

   Set up the equation for mean with x representing the third number, then solve:

   $$mean = \frac{38+43+x}{3} = 45$$

   $$38 + 43 + x = 135$$

   $$x = 54$$

3. What is the median of 24, 27, and 18?

   Place the terms in order, then pick the middle term:

   18, 24, 27

   The median is **24**.

4. What is the median of 24, 27, 18, and 19?

   Place the terms in order. Because there are an even number of terms, the median will be the average of the middle 2 terms:

   18, 19, 24, 27

   $$median = \frac{19+24}{2} = 21.5$$

5. What is the mode of 2, 5, 4, 4, 3, 2, 8, 9, 2, 7, 2, and 2?

   The mode is **2** because it appears the most within the set.

Geometry

Geometry is the study of shapes. On the CHSPE, you'll need to be able to find the perimeter and area of two-dimensional shapes and the volume of three-dimensional shapes. You'll also need to have a basic understanding of congruency and trigonometry.

Properties of Shapes – Area and Perimeter

Area and **perimeter** problems require you to use the equations shown in the table below to find either the area inside a shape or the distance around it (the perimeter). These equations will not be given on the test, so you need to have them memorized on test day.

Shape	Area	Perimeter
circle	$A = \pi r^2$	$C = 2\pi r = \pi d$
triangle	$A = \dfrac{b \times h}{2}$	$P = s_1 + s_2 + s_3$
square	$A = s^2$	$P = 4s$
rectangle	$A = l \times w$	$P = 2l + 2w$

Examples

1. A farmer has purchased 100 meters of fencing to enclose his rectangular garden. If one side of the garden is 20 meters long and the other is 28 meters long, how much fencing will the farmer have left over?

   Answer:

   The perimeter of a rectangle is equal to twice its length plus twice its width:

   $P = 2(20) + 2(28) = 96 \text{ m}$

   The farmer has 100 meters of fencing, so he'll have $100 - 96 = $ **4 meters** left.

2. Taylor is going to paint a square wall that is 3.5 meters high. How much paint will he need?

   Each side of the square wall is 3.5 meters:

   $A = 3.5^2 = \textbf{12.25 m}$

Volume

Volume is the amount of space taken up by a three-dimensional object. Different formulas are used to find the volumes of different shapes.

Shape	Volume
cylinder	$V = \pi r^2 h$
pyramid	$V = \dfrac{l \times w \times h}{3}$
cone	$V = \pi r^2 \dfrac{h}{3}$
sphere	$V = \dfrac{4}{3}\pi r^3$

Examples

1.   Charlotte wants to fill her circular swimming pool with water. The pool has a diameter of 6 meters and is 1 meter deep. How many cubic meters of water will she need to fill the pool?

        Answer:

        This question is asking about the volume of Charlotte's pool.

        The circular pool is actually a cylinder, so use the formula for a cylinder: $V = \pi r^2 h$.

        The diameter is 6 meters. The radius is half the diameter so $r = 6 \div 2 = 3$ meters.

        Now solve for the volume:

$$V = \pi r^2 h$$
$$V = \pi(3 \text{ m})^2(1 \text{ m})$$
$$V = 28.3 \text{ m}^3$$

        Charlotte will need approximately 28.3 cubic meters of water to fill her pool.

2.   Danny has a fishbowl that is filled to the brim with water and purchased some spherical glass marbles to line the bottom of it. He dropped in four marbles, and water spilled out of the fishbowl. If the radius of each marble is 1 centimeter, how much water spilled?

        Answer:

        Since the fishbowl was filled to the brim, the volume of the water that spilled out of it is equal to the volume of the marbles that Danny dropped into it. First, find the volume of one marble using the equation for a sphere:

$$V = \frac{4}{3}\pi r^3$$
$$V = \frac{4}{3}\pi(1 \text{ cm})^3$$
$$V = 4.2 \text{ cm}^3$$

        Since Danny dropped in 4 marbles, multiply this volume by 4 to find the total volume:

$$4.2 \text{ cm}^3 \times 4 = 16.8 \text{ cm}^3$$

        Approximately 16.8 cubic centimeters of water spilled out of the fishbowl.

Circles

The definition of a circle is the set of points that are equal distance from a center point. The distance from the center to any given point on the circle is the **radius**. If you draw a straight line segment across the circle going through the center, the distance along the line segment from one side of the circle to the other is called the **diameter**.

The radius is always equal to half the diameter:

$$d = 2r$$

A **central angle** is formed by drawing radii out from the center to two points A and B along the circle. The **intercepted arc** is the portion of the circle (the arc length) between points A and B. You can find the intercepted arc length l if you know the central angle θ and vice versa:

$$l = 2\pi r \frac{\theta}{360°}$$

A **chord** is a line segment that connects two points on a circle. Unlike the diameter, a chord does not have to go through the center. You can find the chord length if you know either the central angle θ or the radius of the circle r and the distance from the center of the circle to the chord d (d must be at a right angle to the chord):

If you know the central angle, chord length $= 2r \sin \frac{\theta}{2}$

If you know the radius and distance, chord length $= 2\sqrt{r^2 - d^2}$

A **secant** is similar to a chord; it connects two points on a circle. The difference is that a secant is a line, not a line segment, so it extends outside of the circle on either side.

A **tangent** is a straight line that touches a circle at only one point.

A **sector** is the area within a circle that is enclosed by a central angle; if a circle is a pie, a sector is the piece of pie cut by two radii. You can find the **area of a sector** if you know either the central angle θ or the arc length l.

If you know the central angle, the area of the sector $= \pi r^2 \frac{\theta}{360°}$

If you know the arc length, the area of a sector $= \frac{1}{2}rl$

There are two other types of angles you can create in or around a circle. **Inscribed angles** are <u>inside</u> the circle: the vertex is a point P on the circle and the rays extend to two other points on the circle (A and B). As long as A and B remain constant, you can move the vertex P anywhere along the circle and the inscribed angle will be the same. **Circumscribed angles** are <u>outside</u> of the circle: the rays are formed by two tangent lines that touch the circle at points A and B.

You can find the inscribed angle if you know the radius of the circle r and the arc length l between A and B:

inscribed angle $= \dfrac{90°l}{\pi r}$

To find the circumscribed angle, find the central angle formed by the same points A and B and subtract that angle from 180°.

Examples

1. A circle has a diameter of 10 centimeters. What is the intercepted arc length between points A and B if the central angle between those points measures 46°?

    Answer:

    First divide the diameter by two to find the radius:

    $r = 10 \text{ cm} \div 2 = 5 \text{ cm}$

    Now use the formula for intercepted arc length:

    $$l = 2\pi r \frac{\theta}{360°}$$

    $$l = 2\pi(5 \text{ cm}) \frac{46°}{360°}$$

    $$\boldsymbol{l = 4.0 \text{ cm}}$$

2. A chord is formed by line segment $\overline{QP}$. The radius of the circle is 5 cm and the chord length is 6 cm. Find the distance from center C to the chord.

    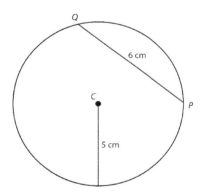

    Answer:

    Use the formula for chord length:

    chord length $= 2\sqrt{r^2 - d^2}$

    In this example, we are told the chord length and the radius, and we need to solve for d:

    $6 \text{ cm} = 2\sqrt{(5 \text{ cm})^2 - d^2}$

    $3 \text{ cm} = \sqrt{(5 \text{ cm})^2 - d^2}$

    $9 \text{ cm}^2 = 25 \text{ cm}^2 - d^2$

    $d^2 = 16 \text{ cm}^2$

    $\boldsymbol{d = 4 \text{ cm}}$

3. Points A and B are located on a circle. The arc length between A and B is 2 centimeters. The diameter of the circle is 8 centimeters. Find the inscribed angle.

Answer:

First, divide the diameter by two to find the radius:

$$r = \frac{1}{2}(8 \text{ cm})$$

$$r = 4 \text{ cm}$$

Now use the formula for an inscribed angle:

$$\text{inscribed angle} = \frac{90°l}{\pi r}$$

$$\text{inscribed angle} = \frac{90°(2 \text{ cm})}{\pi(4 \text{ cm})}$$

inscribed angle = 14.3°

Congruence

Congruence means having the same size and shape. Two shapes are congruent if you can turn (rotate), flip (reflect), and/or slide (translate) one to fit perfectly on top of the other. Two angles are congruent if they measure the same number of degrees; they do not have to face the same direction nor must they necessarily have rays of equal length.

If two triangles have one of the combinations of congruent sides and/or angles listed below, then those triangles are congruent:

SSS – *side, side, side*

ASA – *angle, side, angle*

SAS – *side, angle, side*

AAS – *angle, angle, side*

An **isosceles triangle** has two sides of equal length. The sides of equal length are called the legs and the third side is called the base. If you bisect an isosceles triangle by drawing a line perpendicular to the base, you will form two congruent right triangles.

Where two lines cross and form an X, the opposite angles are congruent and are called **vertical angles**.

Parallel lines are lines that never cross. If you cut two parallel lines by a transversal, you will form four pairs of congruent **corresponding angles**.

109

A **parallelogram** is a quadrilateral in which both pairs of opposite sides are parallel and congruent (of equal length). In a parallelogram, the two pairs of opposite angles are also congruent. If you divide a parallelogram by either of the diagonals, you will form two congruent triangles.

Examples

1. Kate and Emily set out for a bike ride together. They ride 6 miles north, then Kate turns 90° to the west and Emily turns 90° to the east. They both ride another 8 miles. If Kate has 10 more miles to ride home, how far must Emily ride home?

    Answer:

    Draw out Kate's and Emily's trips to see that they form triangles. The triangles have corresponding sides with lengths of 6 miles and 8 miles, and a corresponding angle in between of 90°. This fits the "SAS" rule so the triangles must be congruent. The length Kate has to ride home corresponds to the length Emily has to ride home, so **Emily must ride 10 miles**.

2. Angle *A* measures 53°. Find angle *H*.

    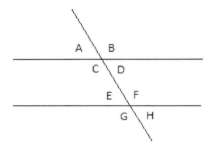

    Answer:

    For parallel lines cut by a transversal, look for vertical and corresponding angles.

    Angles *A* and *D* are vertical angles, so angle *D* must be congruent to angle *A*.
    Angle *D* = 53°.
    Angles *D* and *H* are corresponding angles, so angle *H* must be congruent to angle *D*.
    Angle *H* = 53°.

Right Triangles and Trigonometry

Pythagorean Theorem

Shapes with 3 sides are known as **triangles**. In addition to knowing the formulas for their area and perimeter, you should also know the Pythagorean Theorem, which describes the relationship between the three sides (*a*, *b*, and *c*) of a triangle:

$$a^2 + b^2 = c^2$$

Example

Erica is going to run a race in which she'll run 3 miles due north and 4 miles due east. She'll then run back to the starting line. How far will she run during this race?

Answer:

Start by drawing a picture of Erica's route. You'll see it forms a triangle:

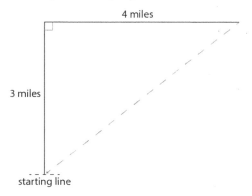

One leg of the triangle is missing, but you can find its length using the Pythagorean Theorem:

$$a^2 + b^2 = c^2$$

$$3^2 + 4^2 = c^2$$

$$25 = c^2$$

$$c = 5$$

Adding all 3 sides gives the length of the whole race:

$$3 + 4 + 5 = \textbf{12 mi}$$

Trigonometry

Using **trigonometry**, you can calculate an angle in a right triangle based on the ratio of two sides of that triangle. You can also calculate one of the side lengths using the measure of an angle and another side. **Sine (sin), cosine (cos)**, and **tangent (tan)** correspond to the three possible ratios of side lengths.

$$\sin\theta = \frac{opposite}{hypotenuse}$$

$$\cos\theta = \frac{adjacent}{hypotenuse}$$

$$\tan\theta = \frac{opposite}{adjacent}$$

Opposite is the side opposite from the angle θ, *adjacent* is the side adjacent to the angle θ, and *hypotenuse* is the longest side of the triangle, opposite from the right angle. SOH-CAH-TOA is an acronym to help you remember which ratio goes with which function.

When solving for a side or an angle in a right triangle, first identify which function to use based on the known lengths or angle.

Examples

1. Phil is hanging holiday lights. To do so safely, he must lean his 20-foot ladder against the outside of his house an angle of 15° or less. How far from the house he can safely place the base of the ladder?

    Answer:

    Draw a triangle with the known length and angle labeled.

    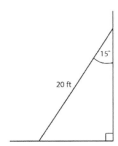

    The known side (the length of the ladder) is the hypotenuse of the triangle, and the unknown distance is the side opposite the angle. Therefore, you can use sine:

    $$\sin \theta = \frac{opposite}{hypotenuse}$$

    $$\sin 15° = \frac{opposite}{20 \text{ feet}}$$

    Now solve for the opposite side:

    $$opposite = \sin 15° \,(20 \text{ feet})$$

    $$\boldsymbol{opposite = 5.2 \text{ feet}}$$

2. Grace is practicing shooting hoops. She is 5 feet 4 inches tall; her basketball hoop is 10 feet high. From 8 feet away, at what angle does she have to look up to see the hoop? Assume that her eyes are 4 inches lower than the top of her head.

    Answer:

    Draw a diagram and notice that the line from Grace's eyes to the hoop of the basket forms the hypotenuse of a right triangle. The side adjacent to the angle of her eyes is the distance from the basket: 8 feet. The side opposite to Grace's eyes is the difference between the height of her eyes and the height of the basket: 10 feet − 5 feet = 5 feet. Next, use the formula for tangent to solve for the angle:

$$\tan\theta = \frac{opposite}{adjacent}$$

$$\tan\theta = \frac{5 \text{ ft}}{8 \text{ ft}}$$

Now take the inverse tangent of both sides to solve for the angle:

$$\theta = \tan^{-1}\frac{5}{8}$$

$$\boldsymbol{\theta = 32°}$$

Coordinate Geometry

Coordinate geometry is the study of points, lines, and shapes that have been graphed on a set of axes.

Points, Lines, and Planes

In coordinate geometry, points are plotted on a **coordinate plane**, a two-dimensional plane in which the **x-axis** indicates horizontal direction and the **y-axis** indicates vertical direction. The intersection of these two axes is the **origin**. Points are defined by their location in relation to the horizontal and vertical axes. The coordinates of a point are written **(x, y)**. The coordinates of the origin are (0, 0). The x coordinates to the right of the origin and the y-coordinates above it are positive; the x-coordinates to the left of the origin and the y-coordinates below it are negative.

A **line** is formed by connecting any two points on a coordinate plane; lines are continuous in both directions. Lines can be defined by their **slope**, or steepness, and their **y-intercept**, or the point at which they intersect the y-axis. A line is represented by the equation $y = mx + b$. The constant m represents slope and the constant b represents the y-intercept.

Examples

1. Matt parks his car near a forest where he goes hiking. From his car he hikes 1 mile north, 2 miles east, then 3 miles west. If his car represents the origin, find the coordinates of Matt's current location.

    Answer:

    To find the coordinates, you must find Matt's displacement along the x- and y-axes. Matt hiked 1 mile north and zero miles south, so his displacement along the y-axis is +1 mile. Matt hiked 2 miles east and 3 miles west, so his displacement along the x axis is +2 miles − 3 miles = −1 mile.

    Matt's coordinates are (−1, 1).

2. A square is drawn on a coordinate plane. The bottom corners are located at $(-2, 3)$ and $(4, 3)$. What are the coordinates for the top right corner?

Answer:

Draw the coordinate plane and plot the given points. If you connect these points you will see that the bottom side is 6 units long. Since it is a square, all sides must be 6 units long. Count 6 units up from the point $(4, 3)$ to find the top right corner.

The coordinates for the top right corner are (4, 9).

The Distance and Midpoint Formulas

To determine the distance between the points (x_1, y_1) and (x_2, y_2) from a grid use the formula $d = \sqrt{(x_2 - x_1)^2 + (y_2 - y_1)^2}$. The midpoint, which is halfway between the 2 points, is the point $\left(\frac{x_1 + x_2}{2}, \frac{y_1 + y_2}{2}\right)$.

Examples

1. What is the distance between points $(3, -6)$ and $(-5, 2)$?

Answer:

Plug the values for $x_1, x_2, y_1,$ and y_2 into the distance formula and simplify:

$$d = \sqrt{(-5 - 3)^2 + (2 - (-6))^2} = \sqrt{64 + 64} = \sqrt{64 \times 2} = \mathbf{8\sqrt{2}}$$

2. What is the midpoint between points $(3, -6)$ and $(-5, 2)$?

Answer:

Plug the values for $x_1, x_2, y_1,$ and y_2 into the midpoint formula and simplify:

$$midpoint = \left(\frac{-5 + 3}{2}, \quad \frac{2 + -6}{2}\right) = \left(\frac{-2}{2}, \frac{4}{2}\right) = \mathbf{(-1, 2)}$$

Area and Perimeter

Area and **perimeter** problems will require you to use the equations shown in the table below to find either the area inside a shape or the distance around it (the perimeter). These equations will not be given on the test, so you need to have them memorized on test day.

EQUATIONS		
shape	area	perimeter
circle	$A = \pi r^2$	$C = 2\pi r = \pi d$
triangle	$A = \frac{b \times h}{2}$	$P = s_1 + s_2 + s_3$
square	$A = s^2$	$P = 4s$
rectangle	$A = l \times w$	$P = 2l + 2w$

Examples

1. A farmer has purchased 100 m of fencing to put around his rectangular garden. If one side of the garden is 20 m long and the other is 28 m, how much fencing will the farmer have left over?

    The perimeter of a rectangle is equal to twice its length plus twice its width:

    P = 2(20) + 2(28) = 96 m

    The farmer has 100 m of fencing, so he'll have

    100 – 96 = **4 m left**

2. Taylor is going to paint a square wall that is 3.5 m tall. What is the total area that Taylor will be painting?

    Each side of the square wall is 3.5 m:

    $A = 3.5^2 = $ **12.25 m²**

Pythagorean Theorem

Shapes with 3 sides are known as **triangles**. In addition to knowing the formulas for their area and perimeter, you should also know the Pythagorean theorem, which describes the relationship between the three sides (*a*, *b*, and *c*) of a right triangle:

$a^2 + b^2 = c^2$

Example

Erica is going to run a race in which she'll run 3 miles due north and 4 miles due east. She'll then run back to the starting line. How far will she run during this race?

One leg of her route (the triangle) is missing, but you can find its length using the Pythagorean theorem:

$a^2 + b^2 = c^2$

$3^2 + 4^2 = c^2$

$25 = c^2$

$c = 5$

Adding all 3 sides gives the length of the whole race:

$3 + 4 + 5 = $ **12 miles**

Graphs and Charts

These questions require you to interpret information from graphs and charts; they are pretty straightforward as long as you pay careful attention to detail. There are several different graph and chart types that may appear on the **CHSPE**.

Bar Graphs

Bar graphs present the numbers of an item that exist in different categories. The categories are shown on the *x*-axis, and the number of items is shown on the *y*-axis. Bar graphs are usually used to easily compare amounts.

Examples

1.

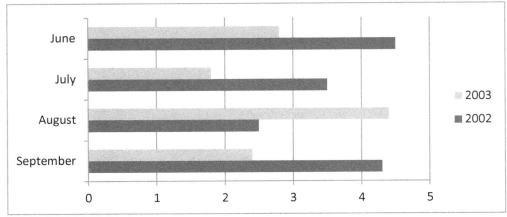

The chart above shows rainfall in inches per month. Which month had the least amount of rainfall? Which had the most?

Answer:

The shortest bar will be the month that had the least rain, and the longest bar will correspond to the month with the greatest amount:

July 2003 had the least, and **June 2002 had the most**.

2.

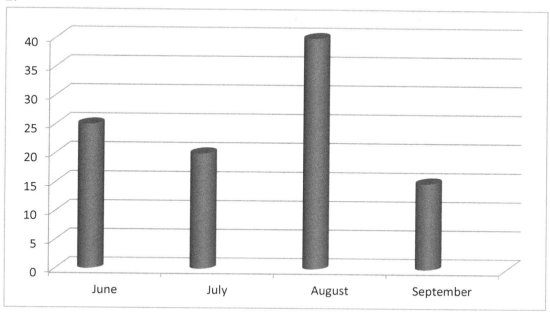

Using the chart above, how many more ice cream cones were sold in July than in September?

Answer:

Tracing from the top of each bar to the scale on the left shows that sales in July were 20 and September sales were 15. So, **5 more cones were sold in July**.

Pie Charts

Pie charts present parts of a whole, and are often used with percentages. Together, all the slices of the pie add up to the total number of items, or 100%.

Example

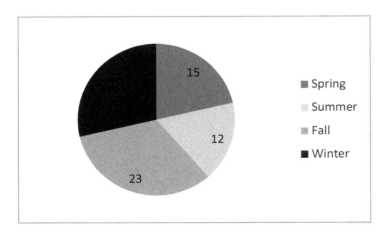

The pie chart above shows the distribution of birthdays in a class of students. How many students have birthdays in the spring or summer?

Answer:

15 students have birthdays in the spring and 12 in winter, so there are **27 students** with birthdays in spring or summer.

Using the same graph above, what percentage of students have birthdays in winter? Use the equation for percent:

$$percent = \frac{part}{whole} = \frac{winter\ birthdays}{total\ birthdays} = \frac{20}{20 + 15 + 23 + 12} = \frac{20}{70} = \frac{2}{7} =$$

.286 or **28.6%**

Line Graphs

Line graphs show trends over time. The number of each item represented by the graph will be on the *y*-axis, and time will be on the *x*-axis.

Example

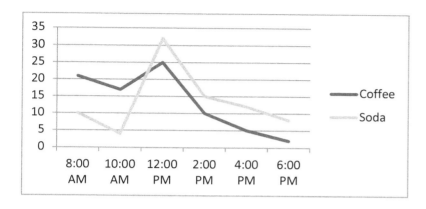

The line graph above shows beverage sales at an airport snack shop throughout the day.

Which beverage sold more at 4:00 p.m.?

Answer:

At 4:00 p.m., approximately 12 sodas and 5 coffees were sold, so more **soda** was sold.

At what time of day were the most beverages sold?

This question is asking for the time of day with the most sales of coffee and soda combined. It is not necessary to add up sales at each time of day to find the answer. Just from looking at the graph, you can see that sales for both beverages were highest at noon, so the answer must be **12:00 p.m.**

Histograms

A **histogram** shows a distribution of a variable in bar chart form. The variables on the *x*-axis is continuous and grouped into categories called bins. The frequency of results in each bin are shown on the *y*-axis. While histograms look like bar graphs, they are more similar to pie charts: they show you parts of a whole.

Example

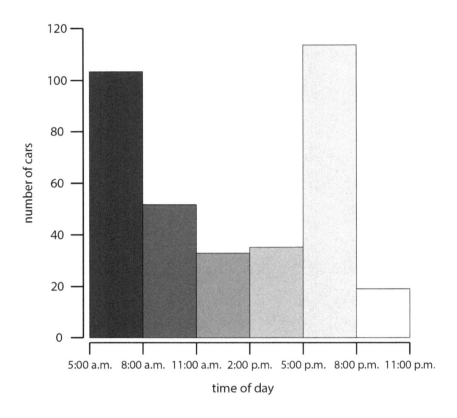

The figure above shows the number of cars that traveled through a toll plaza throughout the day. How many cars passed through the toll plaza between 8:00 a.m. and 5:00 p.m.?

To find the total number, we need to add the number of cars for each relevant time period (note that all number are approximations):

8:00 a.m. – 11:00 a.m.: 50 cars

11:00 a.m. – 2:00 p.m.: 30 cars

2:00 p.m. – 5:00 p.m.: 35 cars

50 + 30 + 35 = **115 cars**

Test Your Knowledge: Mathematics

Numbers and Operations

Types of Numbers

1. Which of the following numbers are integers?

    I. -7

    II. 14.5

    III. $\sqrt{64}$

    A)   I only

    B)   II only

    C)   II and III

    D)   I and III

2. Which of the following is an irrational number?

    A) $9/5$

    B) $\pi/2$

    C) 1.085

    D) 16

3. What kind of number is $-\frac{\sqrt{4}}{17}$?

    A)   whole number

    B)   integer

    C)   rational number

    D)   irrational number

Working with Positive and Negative Numbers

1. Simplify the following expression: $\frac{-24(2)^{-1}}{-3}$

   A) -4

   B)   4

   C) -16

   D) $\frac{1}{144}$

2. Simplify the following inequality: $30 - 9x > -6y$

   A) $-5 + \frac{2}{3}x < y$

   B) $-5 + \frac{2}{3}x > y$

   C) $5 - \frac{2}{3}x < y$

   D) $-5 - \frac{2}{3}x > y$

3. Which of the following is true about negative numbers?

   A)   A negative number raised to a negative number is a positive number.

   B)   A negative number divided by the product of a negative number and a positive number is a positive number.

   C)   The product of a negative number and a positive number, raised to a negative number, is a negative number.

   D)   Both B and C

Order of Operations

1. Solve $\frac{\left(\frac{35}{7}\right)^2 - 3^2}{(7+1)}$

   A)   60.5

   B)   2

   C)   4,227

   D)   20.75

122

2. Solve $(3 + 5)^2 + 24 \div 16 - 5 \div 2$

A)   0.25

B)   30.25

C)   33

D)   63

handwritten: 64 H.5 -2.5 / 65.5 -2.5 / 63

3. Which of the following expressions can be simplified to $8x$?

A) $10 - 2\left(\frac{x^2-x}{x}\right) + 1$

B) $\left(\frac{6+9}{7-4}\right)x + 9 - 6x$

C) $\frac{48}{6\times4} + 2^3x - \frac{4^{(9-6)}}{32}$

D) $16\left(\frac{x^2}{2^{-1}}\right)$

4. Simplify the following expression: $4 - \frac{1}{2^2} + 24 \div (8 + 12)$

A)   4.95

B)   15.28

C)   2.74

D)   1.39

handwritten: $4 - \frac{1}{4} + 24 \div (20)$ / $4 - \frac{1}{4} + 1.2$ / $4 - 0.25 + 1.2$ / 4.95

5. Which of the following statements about order of operations is false?

A)   Operations inside parentheses are simplified before operations outside parentheses.

B)   Multiplication is completed before division.

C)   Exponents are simplified before addition is completed.

D)   Addition and subtraction are completed left to right.

6. Simplify: $\sqrt{(375 + 5^3) - (36 + 64)} - 8$

   A)   28

   B)   4.36

   C)   14.98

   D)   12

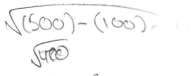

7. Which of the following expressions is equivalent to the expression
   $(2 \times x^2) - (y \div 3)^4 + 5 \div 8^2?$

   A) $2(x^2 - y) \div 3^4 + \left(\frac{5}{8}\right)^2$

   B) $(2x)^2 - \frac{y^4 + 5}{3 + 8^2}$

   C) $2x^2 - \left(\frac{y}{3}\right)^4 + \left(\frac{5}{64}\right)$

   D) $\frac{2x^2 - y}{3^4} + \frac{5}{64}$

8. Simplify: $[56 \div (2 \times 2^2)] - 9 \div 3$

   A)   4

   B) -0.667

   C)   34.33

   D)   109

124

Numbers and Operations Answer Key

Types of Numbers

1. C

2. B

3. D

Working with Positive and Negative Numbers

1. B

2. A

3. D

Order of Operations

1. B

2. D

3. C

4. A

5. B

6. D

7. C

8. A

Units of Measurement

1. Becky is filling her rectangular swimming pool for the summer. The pool is 10 meters long, 6 meters wide, and 1.5 meters deep. How much water will she need to fill the pool?

    A)   90 meters

    B)   90 m²

    C)   90 m³

    D)   90 kilometers

2. Liz got a job wrapping gifts at a department store for the holiday season. To make things more interesting, she has been timing herself to see how quickly she can wrap each gift. Liz can wrap 1 gift in 1 minute and 24 seconds. If it is 10:25:05 a.m. when Liz starts, and she has to wrap 28 gifts before she can take a break, what is the earliest time that Liz will take her break?

    A)   10:59:46 a.m.

    B)   11:04:17 a.m.

    C)   11:59:25 a.m.

    D)   11:04:25 a.m.

3. If a cube with sides 4 centimeters in length weighs 16 grams, what is its density?

    A)   4 grams/centimeters

    B)   2 grams/cm²

    C)   0.25 grams/cm³

    D)   0.0625 grams/cm⁴

4. An ice cube tray has compartments measuring 3 centimeters by 3.5 centimeters by 2 centimeters. How much water (at room temperature) fills each compartment?

    A)   2.1 milliliters

    B)   21 milliliters

    C)   0.21 liters

    D)   2.1 liters

5. Patrick is coming home from vacation in Costa Rica and wants to fill one of his suitcases with bags of Costa Rican coffee. The weight limit for his suitcase is 22 kilograms, and the suitcase itself weighs 3.2 kilograms. If each bag of coffee weighs 800 grams, how many bags can he bring in his suitcase without going over the limit?

A) 27

B) 23

C) 4

D) 2

6. Mark measures his bedroom dimensions, finding them to be 11 feet by 13.5 feet. Find the area of his bedroom in square meters. (1 inch = 2.54 centimeters)

A) 13.796 m²

B) 148.5 m²

C) 3.772 m²

D) 958 m²

7. Anna is buying fruit at the farmers' market. She selects 1.2 kilogram of apples, 800 grams of bananas, and 300 grams of strawberries. The farmer charges her a flat rate of $4 per kilogram. What is the total cost?

A) $4.40

B) $5.24

C) $48.80

D) $9.20

8. Your school has received a foreign exchange student from Ireland. He asks you about the weather forecast for the weekend, and you realize that he is used to hearing temperatures in Celsius. The high temperatures for Saturday and Sunday are 68 °F and 71 °F, respectively. What can you tell him is this weekend's average high temperature in Celsius?
$(^{0}C \times \frac{9}{5} + 32 = {}^{0}F)$

A) 157.1⁰C

B) 20.83⁰C

C) 52.21⁰C

D) 37.5⁰C

9. Ashley has been training for a 10-kilometer race. Her average training pace is 8 minutes and 15 seconds per mile. If she maintains this pace during the race, what will be her finishing time? (1 mile = 5280 feet; 1 foot = 0.3048 meters)

   A)   51:23
   B)   50:53
   C)   51:16
   D)   82:30

10. Years are shorter on Venus because the planet takes only 224.7 Earth days to complete 1 orbit around the sun. How many minutes are in 1 year on Venus?

   A)   323,568 minutes
   B)   525,600 minutes
   C)   19,440,000 minutes
   D)   562 minutes

11. A microsecond (µs) is equal to 1×10^{-6} seconds. Strobe lights typically send out 1 pulse of light every microsecond. If you left a strobe light on for 5 minutes, how many pulses of light would be sent out?

   A) 5×10^6 pulses
   B) 3×10^{-4} pulses
   C)   1800 pulses
   D) 3×10^8 pulses

12. Potatoes are priced at $4.30 per pound. How much does 1620 grams of potatoes cost? (1 kg ≈ 2.2 lbs.)

   A) $15.33
   B) $6.97
   C) $3.17
   D) $0.83

13. Bridget is repainting her rectangular bedroom. Two walls measure 15 feet by 9 feet and the other two measure 12.5 feet by 9 feet. One gallon of paint covers an average of 32 square meters. How many gallons of paint will Bridget use? (1 meter = 3.28 feet)

A)   0.72 gallons

B)   4.72 gallons

C)   15.5 gallons

D)   1.44 gallons

Units of Measurement Answer Key

1. C

2. B

3. C

4. B

5. B

6. A

7. D

8. B

9. C

10. A

11. D

12. A

13. D

Decimals and Fractions

Adding and Subtracting Decimals

1. Simplify: $3.819 + 14.68 + 0.0006$

    A)   18.505

    B)   18.4996

    C)   52.96

    D)   5.2846

2. Simplify: $59.09 - 5.007 - 6.21$

    A)   47.792

    B)   47.81

    C)   47.873

    D)   47.882

3. How many digits are in the sum $951.4 + 98.908 + 1.053$?

    A)   4

    B)   5

    C)   6

    D)   7

Multiplying and Dividing Decimals

1. Simplify: $105.71 \div 31$

    A)   0.341

    B)   3.41

    C)   34.1

    D)   341

2. Simplify: $54.48 \div 0.6$

    A)   0.908

    B)   9.08

    C)   90.8

    D)   908

3. Simplify: 0.08×0.12

    A)   0.0096

    B)   0.096

    C)   0.96

    D)   9.6

Multiplying and Dividing Fractions

1. What is $\frac{4}{9}$ of $\frac{1}{2}$ of $\frac{6}{4}$?

    A) $\frac{1}{3}$

    B) $\frac{64}{3}$

    C) $\frac{12}{18}$

    D) $\frac{2}{9}$

2. $\frac{8}{15}$ is $\frac{1}{6}$ of what number?

    A) $3\frac{1}{15}$

    B) $\frac{15}{48}$

    C) $\frac{4}{45}$

    D) $3\frac{1}{5}$

3. Simplify the expression: $5\frac{2}{3} \times 1\frac{7}{8} \div \frac{1}{3}$

    A) $6\frac{3}{4}$

    B) $31\frac{7}{8}$

    C) $15\frac{3}{4}$

    D) $3\frac{13}{24}$

Adding and Subtracting Fractions

1. Ali, Charlotte, and Katie are selling boxes of candy. The shipment of candy arrives at Ali's house; Ali gives $\frac{4}{15}$ of the boxes to Charlotte and $\frac{3}{10}$ of the boxes to Katie. What fraction of the original shipment is left for Ali?

    A) $\frac{3}{10}$

    B) $\frac{8}{15}$

    C) $\frac{17}{30}$

    D) $\frac{13}{30}$

2. Adam is shopping the clearance section at his favorite department store. He finds a jacket that is marked $\frac{1}{3}$ off. His student discount gives him an additional $\frac{1}{5}$ off the original price. By what fraction is the jacket discounted in total?

    A) $\frac{1}{15}$

    B) $\frac{6}{15}$

    C) $\frac{7}{15}$

    D) $\frac{8}{15}$

3. On Monday, Grace fills the gas tank of her car up to $\frac{3}{4}$ full. On Tuesday, she uses $\frac{1}{8}$ of a tank, on Wednesday she uses $\frac{3}{16}$ of a tank, and on Thursday she uses another $\frac{1}{4}$ of a tank. What fraction of the gas tank is full after Thursday?

A) $\frac{3}{16}$

B) $\frac{7}{16}$

C) $\frac{13}{16}$

D) $\frac{1}{4}$

Converting Fractions to Decimals

1. Based on a favorable performance review at work, Matt receives a $\frac{3}{20}$ increase in his hourly wage. If his original hourly wage is represented by w, express his new wage in decimal form.

A) $0.15w$

B) $0.85w$

C) $1.12w$

D) $1.15w$

2. Express $\frac{15}{25}$ as a decimal.

A)   0.15

B)   0.06

C)   0.6

D)   0.375

3. How many cents is $\frac{8}{11}$ of a dollar?

A)   0.73

B)   0.72

C)   0.81

D)   0.79

Converting Decimals to Fractions

1. Stephanie eats 0.625 of her pizza. If her pizza was cut into 8 slices, how many slices has she eaten?

    A)   3

    B)   4

    C)   5

    D)   6

2. A carnival game involves picking rubber ducks with numbers written on the bottom. There is a 0.05 probability of picking a rubber duck with the number 3. What fraction of the rubber ducks are numbered 3?

    A) $\frac{1}{20}$

    B) $\frac{3}{20}$

    C) $\frac{1}{5}$

    D) $\frac{1}{15}$

3. A chocolate chip cookie recipe calls for 2.375 cups of flour. Express this quantity as a fraction.

    A) $2\frac{3}{5}$ cups

    B) $2\frac{3}{8}$ cups

    C) $2\frac{2}{8}$ cups

    D) $2\frac{1}{3}$ cups

Decimals and Fractions Answer Key

Adding and Subtracting Decimals

1. B
2. C
3. D

Multiplying and Dividing Decimals

1. B
2. C
3. A

Multiplying and Dividing Fractions

1. A
2. D
3. B

Adding and Subtracting Fractions

1. D
2. D
3. A

Converting Fractions to Decimals

1. D
2. C
3. A

Converting Decimals to Fractions

1. C
2. A
3. B

Ratios

1. A marinade recipe calls for 2 tablespoons of lemon juice for $\frac{1}{4}$ cup of olive oil. How much lemon juice should you use with $\frac{2}{3}$ cup olive oil?

   A) $5\frac{1}{3}$ tablespoons

   B) $\frac{3}{4}$ tablespoons

   C) 4 tablespoons

   D) $2\frac{1}{3}$ tablespoons

2. A material's specific heat capacity is the amount of energy needed to increase the temperature of 1 gram of that material by 1 degree Celsius. If the specific heat capacity of aluminum is $0.900\frac{J}{g \cdot °C}$, how many joules of energy does it take to increase the temperature of 2 grams of aluminum by 4 degrees Celsius?

   A) 3.6 joules

   B) 0.1 joules

   C) 7.2 joules

   D) 5.6 joules

3. The density of cork is approximately 0.24 grams per cubic centimeter. How much water would 100 grams of cork displace?

   A) 3.67 cm^3

   B) 1.24 cm^3

   C) 24 cm^3

   D) 4.17 cm^3

4. Stephanie's car uses an average of 29 miles per gallon. $\frac{1}{3}$ of her gas tank holds 3.5 gallons. How many miles can she drive on a full tank of gas?

   A) 33.8 miles

   B) 101.5 miles

   C) 367.5 miles

   D) 304.5 miles

5. Adam owns 4 times as many shirts as he has pairs of pants, and he has 5 pairs of pants for every 2 pairs of shoes. What is the ratio of Adam's shirts to Adam's shoes?

    A)   25 shirts : 1 pair shoes

    B)   10 shirts : 1 pair shoes

    C)   20 shirts : 1 pair shoes

    D)   15 shirts : 2 pairs shoes

6. A box of instant rice provides the following instructions: "For 4 servings, stir 2 cups of rice into 1.75 cups of boiling water." How many cups of water are needed for 6 servings of rice?

    A)   2.625 cups

    B)   13.7 cups

    C)   3 cups

    D)   1.167 cups

7. A restaurant employs servers, hosts, and managers in a ratio of 9:2:1. If there are 36 total employees, how many hosts are there?

    A)   4

    B)   3

    C)   6

    D)   8

8. After a big snow storm, Maria and her brother Bill work together for 3 hours to shovel snow off their driveway and sidewalk. If the total area is 90 square feet, and the snow accumulation is 18 inches, what is the ratio of snow volume shoveled to 1 man hour?

    A)   22.5 ft^3 : 1 man hour

    B)   15 ft^3 : 1 man hour

    C)   270 ft^3 : 1 man hour

    D)   45 ft^3 : 1 man hour

Ratios Answer Key

1. A

2. C

3. D

4. D

5. B

6. A

7. C

8. A

Proportions

1. Megan cuts her birthday cake into 16 pieces. She and her 3 friends each eat a piece. Megan's dad eats $\frac{1}{3}$ of what is remaining. What proportion of the cake is left?

   A) $\frac{13}{24}$

   B) $\frac{1}{2}$

   C) $\frac{1}{4}$

   D) $\frac{3}{4}$

2. A bag contains 30 marbles: $\frac{1}{6}$ are red, $\frac{1}{3}$ are blue, $\frac{1}{5}$ are white, and $\frac{3}{10}$ are black. If 2 white marbles and 1 blue marble are removed, what proportion of marbles left in the bag is blue?

   A) $\frac{2}{9}$

   B) $\frac{1}{6}$

   C) $\frac{5}{14}$

   D) $\frac{1}{3}$

3. A car dealership has sedans, SUVs, and minivans in a ratio of 6:3:1, respectively. In total there are 200 of these vehicles on the lot. What proportion of those vehicles are sedans?

   A) 120

   B) $\frac{3}{100}$

   C) $\frac{3}{5}$

   D) $\frac{3}{10}$

4. If a rare gene mutation is present in $\frac{1}{1,500}$ of the population, and only $\frac{1}{4}$ of those with the mutation show any symptoms, what proportion of the population shows symptoms associated with this mutation?

   A) $\frac{4}{1,500}$

   B) $\frac{1}{6,000}$

   C) $\frac{1}{375}$

   D) $\frac{1}{4,500}$

5. If x represents the proportion of 9th graders in a particular school who are female, and y represents the proportion of students in the school who are 9th graders, what is the expression for the proportion of students in the school who are female 9th graders?

   A) $x + y$

   B) $\frac{x}{y}$

   C) xy

   D) $\frac{y}{x}$

6. In a neighborhood, $\frac{2}{5}$ of the houses are painted yellow. If there are 24 houses that are not painted yellow, how many yellow houses are in the neighborhood?

   A)   16

   B)   9.6

   C)   24

   D)   40

7. If x is the proportion of men who play an instrument, y is the proportion of women who play an instrument, and z is the total number of men, which of the following is true?

   A) $\frac{z}{x}$ = number of men who play an instrument

   B) $(1 - z)x$ = number of men who do not play an instrument

   C) $(1 - x)z$ = number of men who do not play an instrument

   D) $(1 - y)z$ = number of women who do not play an instrument

8. The Robinsons have 3 children, the Sullivans have 1 child, the Jacksons have 2 children, and the Bernsteins have 4 children. What proportion of the children who have more than 1 sibling are Robinsons?

A) $\dfrac{1}{2}$

B) $\dfrac{3}{4}$

C) $\dfrac{7}{10}$

D) $\dfrac{3}{7}$

Proportions Answer Key

1. B

2. D

3. C

4. B

5. C

6. A

7. C

8. D

Percentages

Calculating Percentages

1. 7 is what percent of 60?

    A)   11.67%

    B)   4.20%

    C)   8.57%

    D)   10.11%

2. What percent of 14 is 35?

    A)   4.9%

    B)   2.5%

    C)   40%

    D)   250%

3. 15 is 8 percent of what number?

    A)   1.2

    B)   53.3

    C)   187.5

    D)   120

4. On a given day at the local airport, 15 flights were delayed and 62 left on time. What percentage of the flights was delayed?

    A)   24.2%

    B)   19.5%

    C)   80.5%

    D)   22.4%

5. Gym A offers a monthly membership for 80% of the cost at Gym B; the cost at Gym B is 115% the cost at Gym C. What percentage of the cost at Gym C does Gym A charge?

    A)   35%

    B)   97%

    C)   70%

    D)   92%

6. If there are 380 female students in a graduating class, and male students represent 60% of the graduating class, how many total students are there in the class?

    A)   633

    B)   950

    C)   570

    D)   720

7. What is 18% of 76% of 15,000?

    A)   3,553

    B)   2,052

    C)   633

    D)   8,700

8. A manufacturer sells a product to a retailer for 350% of the production cost. The retailer sells the product to consumers for 600% of the production cost. What percentage of her purchase cost is the retailer's profit when she sells to consumers?

    A)   250%

    B)   41.7%

    C)   58.3%

    D)   71.4%

Percent Change

1. A woman's dinner bill comes to $48.30. If she adds a 20% tip, what will she pay in total?

   A) $9.66

   B) $38.64

   C) $68.30

   D) $57.96

2. A sporting goods store is offering an additional 30% off all clearance items. Angie purchases a pair of running shoes on clearance for $65.00. If the shoes originally cost $85.00, what was her total discount?

   A) 53.5%

   B) 46.5%

   C) 22.9%

   D) 39.2%

3. A car salesman offers you 1 of 2 deals. First, he offers a 15% discount off the total price of the car. As an alternative, he offers a 60 month payment plan, where the payments are reduced by 5% of the previous month's payment every 15 months. Which deal should you choose?

   A) Choose the first deal because you will save 15% vs. 5%.

   B) Choose the second deal because you will save 20% vs. 15%.

   C) Choose the first deal because you will save 15% vs. 7.25%.

   D) The two deals are equivalent.

4. Average winter temperatures have increased approximately 4.5% over the past 100 years. If the average winter temperature in 2015 is 34 °F, what was the average winter temperature in 1915?

   A) 1.5 °F

   B) 32.5 °F

   C) 35.5 °F

   D) 29.5 °F

5. In July, gas prices increased by 15%. In August, they decreased by 10%. What is the total percent change since June?

    A) 5% increase

    B) 3.5% decrease

    C) 3.5% increase

    D) 1.5% increase

6. Toledo has been working full time but would like to cut back to part time. He normally works from 9:00 a.m. to 5:00 p.m. Monday through Friday. Now he leaves at 1:00 p.m. on Tuesdays and Thursdays. By what percentage has he decreased his weekly work hours?

    A) 20%

    B) 25%

    C) 30%

    D) 80%

7. Andre puts $5,000 in a compounding-interest savings account. Every month, he makes 1.25% interest on his balance (and this interest is compounded so that the added amount also earns interest the following month). What will his account balance be after 3 months?

    A) $187.50

    B) $5,187.50

    C) $189.85

    D) $5,189.85

8. The number of college applicants increased in 2014 by 7%. This is 15% larger than the increase in 2013. What was the percentage increase in college applicants in 2013?

    A) 2%

    B) 6%

    C) 8%

    D) 4%

Percentages Answer Key

Calculating Percentages

1. A

2. D

3. C

4. B

5. D

6. B

7. B

8. D

Percent Change

1. D

2. B

3. C

4. B

5. B

6. A

7. D

8. B

Comparison of Rational Numbers

1. Put the following integers and fractions in order from smallest to largest: $0.125, \frac{6}{9}, \frac{1}{7}, 0.60$

    A) $\frac{1}{7}, 0.125, \frac{6}{9}, 0.60$

    B) $\frac{1}{7}, 0.125, 0.60, \frac{6}{9}$

    C) $0.125, \frac{1}{7}, 0.60, \frac{6}{9}$

    D) $\frac{1}{7}, 0.125, \frac{6}{9}, 0.60$

2. Jess and Joe both took a math exam. Jess answered $\frac{7}{8}$ of the questions correctly. Joe answered 88% correctly. Who scored higher on the exam and by how much?

    A)   Jess by 0.5%

    B)   Joe by 0.5%

    C)   Jess by $\frac{1}{16}$

    D)   Joe by $\frac{1}{16}$

3. Put the following fractions in order from smallest to largest: $\frac{2}{16}, \frac{1}{24}, \frac{3}{32}, \frac{3}{16}, \frac{5}{48}$

    A) $\frac{1}{24} < \frac{3}{32} < \frac{5}{48} < \frac{2}{16} < \frac{3}{16}$

    B) $\frac{1}{24} < \frac{5}{48} < \frac{3}{32} < \frac{2}{16} < \frac{3}{16}$

    C) $\frac{1}{24} < \frac{3}{32} < \frac{2}{16} < \frac{3}{16} < \frac{5}{48}$

    D) $\frac{1}{24} < \frac{2}{16} < \frac{3}{32} < \frac{3}{16} < \frac{5}{48}$

4. 4 friends shared a pizza. Adam ate $\frac{1}{5}$ of the pizza, Patrick ate $\frac{3}{14}$, David ate $\frac{2}{15}$ and Jay ate $\frac{3}{16}$. Who ate the most pizza?

    A)   Adam

    B)   Patrick

    C)   David

    D)   Jay

5. Order the following quantities on a number line, from most negative to most positive:

$2^{-1}, -\frac{4}{3}, (-1)^3, \frac{2}{5}$

A) $2^{-1}, -\frac{4}{3}, (-1)^3, \frac{2}{5}$

B) $-\frac{4}{3}, (-1)^3, 2^{-1}, \frac{2}{5}$

C) $-\frac{4}{3}, \frac{2}{5}, 2^{-1}, (-1)^3$

D) $-\frac{4}{3}, (-1)^3, \frac{2}{5}, 2^{-1}$

Comparison of Rational Numbers Answer Key

1. C

2. B

3. A

4. B

5. D

Exponents and Radicals

1. Simplify the expression $x^5 \times x^9 - x^2$.

    A) x^{43}

    B) $x^{14} - x^2$

    C) x^{12}

    D) $3x^{43}$

2. Simplify the expression $5(x^2)^{10}$.

    A) $5x^{20}$

    B) $5x^{12}$

    C) $5\,x^{-8}$

    D) $50x^2$

3. Simplify the expression $\dfrac{x^5}{(x^2)^{-1}}$.

    A) x^3

    B) $x^{3/2}$

    C) $\dfrac{1}{x^{3/2}}$

    D) x^7

4. Simplify: $\left(x^{1/2}\right)^{-3}$

    A) $x^{-1/2}$

    B) $x^{-5/2}$

    C) $\dfrac{1}{\sqrt{x^3}}$

    D) $\sqrt{x^3}$

5. Simplify: $\sqrt[3]{\dfrac{64}{x}} - \dfrac{1}{\sqrt[3]{x}}$

A) $\dfrac{3}{\sqrt[3]{x}}$

B) $\dfrac{4}{\sqrt[3]{x}}$

C) $3x^{-3}$

D) $4x^{-3}$

Exponents and Radicals Answer Key

1. B

2. A

3. D

4. C

5. A

Algebra

Evaluating Algebraic Expressions

1. Evaluate the expression $\frac{4x}{x-1}$ when $x = 5$.

   A)   3

   B)   4

   C)   5

   D)   6

2. Evaluate the expression $\frac{x^2-2y}{y}$ when $x = 20$ and $y = \frac{x}{2}$.

   A)   0

   B)   38

   C)   36

   D)   19

3. Evaluate the expression $\sqrt{(x^{-1})4x}$ when $x = y + 3$ and $y = 14$.

   A)   2

   B) -2

   C)   34

   D) $\frac{1}{\sqrt{2}}$

Adding and Subtracting Algebraic Expressions

1. Simplify: $3x^3 + 4x - (2x + 5y) + y$

   A) $3x^3 + 2x + y$

   B) $11x - 4y$

   C) $3x^3 + 2x - 4y$

   D) $29x - 4y$

2. Find the sum: $2\left(\frac{y}{x}\right) + \frac{1}{x}(3y)$

   A) $\frac{y}{x}$

   B) $\frac{5y}{x^2}$

   C) $\frac{5y}{6x}$

   D) $\frac{5y}{x}$

3. Simplify the expression: $x^3 - 3x^2 + (2x)^3 - x$

   A) $x^3 - 3x^2 + 7x$

   B) $9x^3 - 3x^2 - x$

   C) $20x$

   D) $7x^3 - 3x^2 - x$

Multiplying and Dividing Algebraic Expressions

1. Multiply the following terms: $(11xy)(2x^2y)$

   A) $13xy + x$

   B) $22x^3y^2$

   C) $44x^3y^3$

   D) $22xy^2 + 2x^2$

2. Simplify the expression $\frac{(4xy)^3}{x^5y}$.

   A) $\frac{12}{x^4}$

   B) $12x^2y^2$

   C) $64x^2y^2$

   D) $\frac{64y^2}{x^2}$

3. Simplify the expression: $\frac{(x^a y^b)(z^b y^a)}{z(xy)^a}$.

    A) $y^b z^{(b-1)}$

    B) $xy^b z^{(b-1)}$

    C) $xy^{ab} z$

    D) $\frac{y^b}{z^b}$

Factoring Expressions

1. Factor the expression $100x^2 + 25x$.

    A) $100x(x + 25x)$

    B) $25(4x + x)$

    C) $25x(4x + 1)$

    D) $25(4x^2 + x)$

2. Factor the expression $9x^2 + 42xy + 49y^2$.

    A) $(3x - 7y)^2$

    B) $(3x + 7y)^2$

    C) $(3x + 7)(x + y)$

    D) $(3x + 7y)(3x - 7)$

3. Factor the expression $64 - 100x^2$.

    A) $(8 + 10x)(8 - 10x)$

    B) $(8 + 10x)^2$

    C) $(8 - 10x)^2$

    D) $(8 + 10x)(8x + 10)$

Algebra Answer Key

Evaluating Algebraic Expressions

1. C

2. B

3. A

Adding and Subtracting Algebraic Expressions

1. C

2. D

3. B

Multiplying and Dividing Algebraic Expressions

1. B

2. D

3. A

Factoring Expressions

1. C

2. B

3. A

Linear Equations

Solving Linear Equations

1. Solve for a: $3a + 4 = 2a$

   A) $a = -4$

   B) $a = 4$

   C) $a = \frac{-4}{5}$

   D) $a = \frac{4}{5}$

2. Solve for x: $x \div 7 = x - 36$

   A) $x = 6$

   B) $x = -6$

   C) $x = 42$

   D) $x = 252$

3. Solve for y: $10y - 8 - 2y = 4y - 22 + 5y$

   A) $y = -4\frac{2}{3}$

   B) $y = 14$

   C) $y = 30$

   D) $y = -30$

4. Solve for b: $2(b + 4.8) = 11b - 1.2$

   A) $b = 1.2$

   B) $b = 4.5$

   C) $b = 5.4$

   D) $b = 0.6$

5. Solve for x: $8(x + 5) = -3x - 48$

    A) $x = 0.625$

    B) $x = 12.8$

    C) $x = 8$

    D) $x = -8$

6. Solve for x: $8x - 6 = 3x + 24$

    A) $x = 3.6$

    B) $x = 5$

    C) $x = 6$

    D) $x = 2.5$

7. Solve for x: $15x - 4y + 4 = 3x - 2(2y + 1)$

    A) $x = \frac{1}{2}$

    B) $x = -\frac{1}{2}$

    C) $x = 6$

    D) $x = -6$

8. Solve for x: $\frac{3}{x} + \frac{2}{3} = \frac{8}{x} + \frac{1}{9}$

    A) $x = 9$

    B) $x = 7$

    C) $x = 6$

    D) $x = -9$

Graphing Linear Equations

1. Find the slope of the line that passes through points $(-1,4)$ and $(3,12)$.

   A) $m = 2$

   B) $m = 1\frac{4}{5}$

   C) $m = \frac{5}{9}$

   D) $m = \frac{1}{2}$

2. The slope of a straight line is -3 and the y-intercept is -2. Find the x-intercept.

   A) $x = 1\frac{1}{2}$

   B) $x = -2$

   C) $x = -\frac{2}{3}$

   D) $x = -3$

3. Find the equation for the line that passes through the points $(2,7)$ and $(6,10)$.

   A) $y = \frac{4}{5}x - 5\frac{1}{2}$

   B) $y = \frac{3}{4}x + 5\frac{1}{2}$

   C) $y = 1\frac{1}{3}x + 2$

   D) $y = 1\frac{1}{3}x - 4\frac{1}{2}$

Systems of Equations

1. Use the equation $y = 4x - 16$ to solve for x when $y = 4$.

   A) $x = 5$

   B) $x = -5$

   C) $x = 0$

   D) $x = 4$

2. What is the value of y if $x > 0$: $4x - \frac{y}{3} = -2$ and $\frac{6}{x} = 24x$

    A) $y = \frac{1}{2}$

    B) $y = 3$

    C) $y = 12$

    D) $y = -4$

3. Solve for x: $21x + 4.5 = 3y$ and $18x - 3 = 2y$

    A) $x = 3.5$

    B) $x = 7.5$

    C) $x = 2.5$

    D) $x = 1.5$

4. Solve for x and y: $4x + 3y = 10$ and $2x - y = 20$

    A) $(x, y) = (3, -4)$

    B) $(x, y) = (6, -7)$

    C) $(x, y) = (7, -6)$

    D) $(x, y) = (3, -2)$

5. Solve for x and y: $15x + 2y = 3$ and $12x + y = -3$

    A) $(x, y) = (-1, 9)$

    B) $(x, y) = (1, -15)$

    C) $(x, y) = (1, -6)$

    D) $(x, y) = (-\frac{1}{6}, -1)$

Building Equations

1. Jane earns $15 per hour babysitting. If she starts out with $275 in her bank account, which of the following equations represents how many hours will she have to babysit for her account to reach $400?

   A) $-400 = 15h - 275$

   B) $400 = \frac{15}{h} + 275$

   C) $400 = 15h$

   D) $400 = 15h + 275$

2. If m represents a car's average mileage in miles per gallon, p represents the price of gas in dollars per gallon, and d represents a distance in miles, which of the following algebraic equations represents the cost (c) of gas per mile?

   A) $c = \frac{dp}{m}$

   B) $c = \frac{p}{m}$

   C) $c = \frac{mp}{d}$

   D) $c = \frac{m}{p}$

3. At a bake sale, muffins are priced at $1.50 each and cookies are priced at $1 for two. If 11 muffins are sold, and the total money earned is $29.50, how many cookies were sold?

   A)   12

   B)   13

   C)   23

   D)   26

4. A bag contains twice as many red marbles as blue marbles, and the number of blue marbles is 88% of the number of green marbles. If g represents the number of green marbles, which of the following expressions represents the total number of marbles in the bag?

   A) $3.88g$

   B) $3.64g$

   C) $2.64g$

   D) $2.32g$

163

5. A cleaning company charges $25 per hour per room. Added to this charge is a 7% sales tax. If t represents the number of hours and r represents the number of rooms, which of the following algebraic equations represents the total cost c of cleaning?

A) $c = 25.07(t)(r)$

B) $c = 32.00(t)(r)$

C) $c = 26.75(t)(r)$

D) $c = \dfrac{26.75(t)}{(r)}$

Linear Equations Answer Key

Solving Linear Equations

1. A
2. C
3. B
4. A
5. D
6. C
7. B
8. A

Graphing Linear Equations

1. A
2. C
3. B

Systems of Equations

1. A
2. C
3. D
4. C
5. A

Building Equations

1. D
2. B
3. D
4. B
5. C

Linear Inequalities

Solving Linear Inequalities

1. Solve for x: $4x + 3 > -9$

    A) $x < 3$

    B) $x > -3$

    C) $x > -1\frac{1}{2}$

    D) $x < 1\frac{1}{2}$

2. Solve for x: $6x + 5 \geq -15 + 8x$

    A) $x \leq 10$

    B) $x \leq -5$

    C) $x \leq 5$

    D) $x \leq 20$

3. Solve for x: $2(-3x - 2) < 2$

    A) $x > -2$

    B) $x < -\frac{2}{3}$

    C) $x < -1$

    D) $x > -1$

4. Find all possible values of x given the following equations: $16 - x \leq 7x$ and $2x - 40 < 6$

    A) $2 < x \leq 23$

    B) $2\frac{2}{3} \leq x < 23$

    C) $2 \leq x < 23$

    D) $2 \leq x > -10$

5. 5 subtracted from 3 times x is greater than x subtracted from 15. Solve this inequality for x.

A) $x < -5$

B) $x > 5$

C) $x > 10$

D) $x > -10$

Graphing Linear Inequalities

1. Find the slope of the line for the graph of the inequality $4 - \frac{y}{2} < 3x + 1$

A) -6

B) 6

C) -3

D) $-1\frac{1}{2}$

2. A solid line passes through the points $(0,2)$ and $(2,8)$, and the graph is shaded above the line. What is the inequality statement for this graph?

A) $y < 6x + 2$

B) $y \leq 3x$

C) $y > 3x + 2$

D) $y \geq 3x + 2$

3. At what point does the graph of the inequality $2y + 4 < -2x - 6$ intersect the y-axis?

A) $(-5,0)$

B) $(0,-1)$

C) $(0,-5)$

D) $(0,-10)$

Linear Inequalities Answer Key

Solving Linear Inequalities

1. B

2. A

3. D

4. C

5. B

Graphing Linear Inequalities

1. A

2. D

3. C

Quadratic Equations

Solving Quadratic Equations

1. Solve for x: $(2x + 6)(3x - 15) = 0$

   A) $x = -5, 3$

   B) $x = -3, 5$

   C) $x = -2, -3$

   D) $x = -6, 15$

2. Solve for x: $-15x^2 = 12x$

   A) $x = \frac{1}{\sqrt{15}}, \frac{1}{12}$

   B) $x = 0, -\frac{4}{5}$

   C) $x = 0, -3$

   D) $x = 0, 1\frac{1}{4}$

3. Solve for x: $16x^2 + 8x + 1 = 0$

   A) $x = -\frac{1}{4}$

   B) $x = -\frac{1}{4}, \frac{1}{4}$

   C) $x = -4, 4$

   D) $x = 1, 4$

4. Solve for x: $x^2 + 7x = -8$

   A) $x = 0, -7$

   B) $x = 5, -12$

   C) $x = -4.94, -9.06$

   D) $x = -1.44, -5.54$

5. Solve for x: $-4x^2 + 15 = 40x$

   A) $x = -9.6, -0.39$

   B) $x = -10.36, 0.36$

   C) $x = 2.9, 82.9$

   D) $x = -6.64, 6.64$

Graphing Quadratic Equations

1. Find the vertex of the parabola given by the function $f(x) = 4x^2 - 2x + 10$.

   A) $(1, 12)$

   B) $(-1, 16)$

   C) $(0.25, 9.75)$

   D) $(-0.25, 10.75)$

2. A parabola has a vertex at $(1, -4)$ and passes through the point $(-1, 8)$. Find the equation of the function.

   A) $f(x) = 4(x - 3)^2 + 1$

   B) $f(x) = 3x^2 - 4x + 1$

   C) $f(x) = (x + 4)^2 - 1$

   D) $f(x) = 3(x - 1)^2 - 4$

3. Consider the quadratic function $f(x) = -x^2 + 5x - 15$. Which of the following statements is true about the graph of this function?

   A) The parabola is upward-facing with a vertex at $(2.5, -8.75)$.

   B) The parabola is downward-facing with a vertex at $(2.5, -8.75)$.

   C) The parabola is upward-facing with a vertex at $(-2.5, -33.75)$.

   D) The parabola is downward-facing with a vertex at $(-2.5, -33.75)$.

Quadratic Equations Answer Key

Solving Quadratic Equations

1. B

2. B

3. A

4. D

5. B

Graphing Quadratic Equations

1. C

2. D

3. B

Quadratic Inequalities

1. Solve for x: $x^2 - 9 < 0$.

   A) $x > 3, x < -3$

   B) $-3 < x < 3$

   C) $x > 3$

   D) $x < -3$

2. Solve for x: $4x^2 - 2x > 6$

   A) $-2 < x < 3$

   B) $-3 < x < 2$

   C) $x < -1, x > 1.5$

   D) $-1 < x < 1.5$

3. Solve for x: $72x^2 > 36x$

   A) $x > 0.5, x < 0$

   B) $0 < x < 0.5$

   C) $x < 0$

   D) $0 < x < 2$

Quadratic Inequalities Answer Key

1. B

2. C

3. A

Functions

Describing Functions

1. What is the range of the function $f(x) = x^2 + 2$?

   A) all real numbers

   B) all real numbers greater than 2

   C) all real numbers greater than or equal to 2

   D) all real numbers less than or equal to 2

2. Consider the function $f(x) = -2x - 5$ with the range $\{17, 15, 11, -5\}$. Define the domain.

   A) domain $= \{-11, -10, -8, 0\}$

   B) domain $= \{-39, -35, -27, 5\}$

   C) domain $= \{-14, -11, -6, 0\}$

   D) domain $= \{-6, -5, -3, 5\}$

3. Which of the following is always true of functions?

   A) For each value in the range, there is only one value in the domain.

   B) For each value in the domain, there is only one value in the range.

   C) The range of a function includes all real numbers.

   D) The domain of a function includes all real numbers.

Exponential Functions

1. If $f(x) = 3^x - 2$, evaluate $f(5)$.

   A) 27

   B) 243

   C) 241

   D) 13

2. Which of the following is true of the function $f(x) = 8^x$?

   A) The graph of the function has a horizontal asymptote along the negative x-axis.

   B) The graph of the function has a horizontal asymptote along the positive x-axis.

   C) The graph of the function has a vertical asymptote along the negative y-axis.

   D) The graph of the function has a vertical asymptote along the positive y-axis.

3. If $f(x) = 0.5^x + 1$, evaluate $f(-2)$.

   A) 0.75

   B) 2

   C) 4

   D) 5

4. If $f(x) = e^{2x}$, evaluate $\ln[f(3)]$.

   A) 3

   B) 5

   C) 6

   D) $\frac{1}{e^6}$

5. Which of the following is true of the function $f(x) = 1^x - 3$?

   A) The graph of the function is a horizontal line at $y = -2$.

   B) The graph of the function is a vertical line at $x = -2$.

   C) The graph of the function has a horizontal asymptote at $y = -3$.

   D) The graph of the function has a vertical asymptote at $x = -3$.

Logarithmic Functions

1. If $f(x) = \log_3 x$, evaluate $f(81)$.

    A)   2

    B)   4

    C)   9

    D)   27

2. If $f(x) = \log_x 64$, evaluate $f(4)$.

    A)   2

    B)   3

    C)   4

    D)   16

3. If $f(x) = \ln x$, evaluate $f(e^{-5})$.

    A) $\dfrac{1}{e^5}$

    B) $\dfrac{1}{5}$

    C) -5

    D)   5

4. Which of the following is true of the function $f(x) = \log_{1/2} x$?

    A)   The graph of the function has a horizontal asymptote along the negative x-axis.

    B)   The graph of the function has a horizontal asymptote along the positive x-axis.

    C)   The graph of the function has a vertical asymptote along the negative y-axis.

    D)   The graph of the function has a vertical asymptote along the positive y-axis.

5. If $f(x) = \log_x 32$, for what value of x does $f(x) = 5$?

   A) $x = 2$

   B) $x = 6.4$

   C) $x = 33,554,432$

   D) $x = 1.05$

Arithmetic and Geometric Sequences

1. Find the next term in the following sequence: $5, 12, 19, 26, ...$

   A)   35

   B)   37

   C)   33

   D)   34

2. Find the 10th term in the following sequence: $20, 8, -4, -16, ...$

   A) -100

   B) -88

   C) -72

   D) -136

3. Find the common ratio of the following sequence: $\frac{1}{12}, \frac{1}{4}, \frac{3}{4}, 2\frac{1}{4}, ...$

   A)   3

   B) $\frac{1}{3}$

   C) $\frac{1}{4}$

   D) $\frac{3}{4}$

4. Find the nth term in the following sequence: $11, 7, 3, -1, ...$

    A) $a_n = 11 + 4(n-1)$

    B) $a_n = 11(4)^{(n-1)}$

    C) $a_n = 15 - 4n$

    D) $a_n = 11 - 4n$

5. Find the common ratio for a geometric sequence with terms $a_1 = -2$ and $a_6 = 486$.

    A) -6

    B) -2.5

    C) 40.5

    D) -3

Functions Answer Key

Describing Functions

1. C

2. A

3. B

Exponential Functions

1. C

2. A

3. D

4. C

5. A

Logarithmic Functions

1. B

2. B

3. C

4. D

5. A

Arithmetic and Geometric Sequences

1. C

2. B

3. A

4. C

5. D

Absolute Value

1. Evaluate the expression $|3x - y| + |2y - x|$ if $x = -4$ and $y = -1$.

    A) -11

    B) 11

    C) 13

    D) -13

2. If $f(x) = |x - 28|$, evaluate $f(-12)$.

    A) -16

    B) 40

    C) 16

    D) -40

3. For which of the following functions does $f(x) = |f(x)|$ for every value of x?

    A) $f(x) = 3 - x$

    B) $f(x) = 2x + x^2$

    C) $f(x) = x^3 + 1$

    D) $f(x) = x^2 + (2 - x)^2$

4. Consider the equations $|3x - 5| = 23$ and $|10 + 4y| = 12$. If x and y are both negative numbers, what is $|y - x|$?

    A) 0.5

    B) 7.33

    C) 4

    D) 8

5. If $|8x - 2| < 4$, which of the following is true of x?

A) $-0.75 < x < 0.25$

B) $-0.25 < x < 0.75$

C) $0.25 < x < 0.75$

D) $x > 0$

Absolute Value Answer Key

1. C

2. B

3. D

4. A

5. A

Matrices

1. Simplify: $\begin{bmatrix} 2 & -3 & 12 \\ 10 & 1 & -8 \end{bmatrix} + \begin{bmatrix} 6 & 7 & -9 \\ -1 & 3 & 5 \end{bmatrix}$

   A) $\begin{bmatrix} 8 & 10 & 3 \\ 11 & 4 & 3 \end{bmatrix}$

   B) $\begin{bmatrix} 16 & -21 & -108 \\ -10 & 3 & -40 \end{bmatrix}$

   C) $\begin{bmatrix} 20 & 2 & 4 \\ 5 & 10 & 4 \end{bmatrix}$

   D) $\begin{bmatrix} 8 & 4 & 3 \\ 9 & 4 & -3 \end{bmatrix}$

2. Simplify: $\begin{bmatrix} 11 \\ 8 \\ 3 \end{bmatrix} - \begin{bmatrix} 15 \\ -4 \\ 9 \end{bmatrix}$

   A) $\begin{bmatrix} 4 \\ 12 \\ -6 \end{bmatrix}$

   B) $\begin{bmatrix} 4 \\ 4 \\ 6 \end{bmatrix}$

   C) $\begin{bmatrix} -4 \\ -12 \\ 6 \end{bmatrix}$

   D) These matrices cannot be subtracted as written.

3. Simplify: $5\begin{bmatrix} 2 & 6 \\ 1 & 0 \end{bmatrix} + 3\begin{bmatrix} 5 & 1 \\ 2 & 9 \end{bmatrix}$

   A) $\begin{bmatrix} 10 & 30 \\ 5 & 0 \end{bmatrix}$

   B) $\begin{bmatrix} -5 & 27 \\ -1 & -27 \end{bmatrix}$

   C) $\begin{bmatrix} 15 & 3 \\ 6 & 27 \end{bmatrix}$

   D) $\begin{bmatrix} 25 & 33 \\ 11 & 27 \end{bmatrix}$

4. If A = [−5 2 4] and B = $\begin{bmatrix} 0 & -3 \\ 10 & -6 \\ 7 & -1 \end{bmatrix}$, what is AB?

A)   [48 −1]

B)   [40 0]

C) $\begin{bmatrix} 15 \\ 8 \\ 24 \end{bmatrix}$

D)   [85 34 68]

5. If A = $\begin{bmatrix} 2 & -1 & 0 \\ 3 & 5 & 1 \end{bmatrix}$ and B = $\begin{bmatrix} 4 & -2 \\ 5 & 6 \\ 3 & 0 \end{bmatrix}$, what is AB?

A) $\begin{bmatrix} 8 & -5 & 0 \\ -6 & 30 & 0 \end{bmatrix}$

B) $\begin{bmatrix} 3 & -10 \\ 40 & 24 \end{bmatrix}$

C) $\begin{bmatrix} -4 & -6 & 0 \\ 12 & 25 & 3 \end{bmatrix}$

D) $\begin{bmatrix} 8 & 12 \\ 40 & 24 \end{bmatrix}$

Matrices Answer Key

1. D

2. A

3. D

4. A

5. B

Geometry – Properties of Shapes

Area and Perimeter

1. Find the area of a rectangular athletic field that is 100 meters long and 45 meters wide.

   A)   290 meters

   B)   4,500 m^2

   C)   145 m^2

   D)   4.5 km^2

2. Melissa is ordering fencing to enclose a square area of 5625 square feet. How many feet of fencing does she need?

   A)   75 feet

   B)   150 feet

   C)   300 feet

   D)   5,625 feet

3. Adam is painting a 4-walled shed. The shed is 5 feet wide, 4 feet deep, and 7 feet high. How much paint will Adam need?

   A)   126 ft^2

   B)   140 ft^3

   C)   63 ft^2

   D)   46 feet

4. James is building an octagonal gazebo with equal sides in his backyard. If one side is 5.5 feet wide, what is the perimeter of the entire gazebo?

   A)   22 feet

   B)   30.25 feet

   C)   44 feet

   D)   242 feet

5. A courtyard garden has flower beds in the shape of 4 equilateral triangles arranged so that their bases enclose a square space in the middle for a fountain. Each flower bed has paving stones lining its entire triangular perimeter. If the space for the fountain has an area of 1 square meter, calculate the total distance lined by the paving stones.

   A)   2 meters

   B)   6 meters

   C)   9 meters

   D)   12 meters

6. A courtyard garden has flower beds in the shape of 4 equilateral triangles arranged so that their bases enclose a square space in the middle for a fountain. If the space for the fountain has an area of 1 square meter, find the total area of the flower beds and fountain space.

   A)   1.73 m²

   B)   2.73 m²

   C)   1.43 m²

   D)   3 m²

7. 2 identical circles are drawn next to each other with their sides just touching; both circles are enclosed in a rectangle whose sides are tangent to the circles. If each circle's radius is 2 inches, find the area of the rectangle.

   A)   24 cm²

   B)   8 cm²

   C)   32 cm²

   D)   16 cm²

8. A grain silo is cylinder-shaped with a height of 10 meters and a diameter of 3.2 meters. What is the surface area of the silo, including the top but not the base?

   A)   233.23 m²

   B)   265.40 m²

   C)   116.61 m²

   D)   108.57 m²

9. Find the total surface area of a box that is 12 inches long, 18 inches wide, and 6 inches high.

   A)   144 in^2

   B)   1,296 in^3

   C)   792 in^2

   D)   396 in^2

10. A developer is designing a rectangular parking lot for a new shopping center. A 20-foot-wide driving lane circles the interior, which has 6 rows of parking spaces divided by 5 driving lanes. Each row of parking spaces is 36 feet wide and 90 feet long. The driving lanes are 20 feet wide and 90 feet long. What is the perimeter of the entire parking lot?

   A)   972 feet

   B)   486 feet

   C)   812 feet

   D)   852 feet

Volume

1. A cylindrical canister is 9 inches high and has a diameter of 5 inches. What is the maximum volume this canister can hold?

   A)   176.7 in^2

   B)   45 in^2

   C)   141.4 in^2

   D)   706.9 in^2

2. If a spherical water balloon is filled with 113 milliliters of water, what is the approximate radius of the balloon?

   A)   4.0 centimeters

   B)   3.0 centimeters

   C)   3.6 centimeters

   D)   3.3 centimeters

3. A particular hourglass is made from 2 cones. The diameter of the base of each cone is 3 centimeters, and the height of the 2 cones combined is 12 centimeters. If the hourglass holds 4 milliliters of sand, how much empty space remains inside the hourglass?

A) 4.5 cm³

B) 0.5 cm³

C) 5 cm³

D) 9 cm³

4. 5 pennies are dropped into a fountain. If each penny measures 19 millimeters in diameter and is 1.5 millimeters thick, how much water is displaced?

A) 425.3 mm³

B) 2.1 cm³

C) 676.9 mm³

D) 4.3 cm³

5. A packing box holds 1.5 cubic feet. If the box is as long as it is wide, and measures 18 inches in height, what is its width?

A) 6 inches

B) 18 inches

C) 12 inches

D) 1 inches

Circles

1. A circular swimming pool has a circumference of 49 feet. What is the diameter of the pool?

A) 15.6 feet

B) 12.3 feet

C) 7.8 feet

D) 17.8 feet

2. A pizza has a diameter of 10 inches. If you cut a slice with a central angle of 40 degrees, how many inches of crust does that slice include?

    A)   31.4 inches

    B)   7.0 inches

    C)   3.5 inches

    D)   3.3 inches

3. A pizza has a diameter of 10 inches. If you cut a slice with a central angle of 40 degrees, what will be the surface area of the pizza slice?

    A)   9.2 in^2

    B)   8.7 in^2

    C)   3.5 in^2

    D)   17.4 in^2

4. Bryan drives up to a traffic circle from Elm Street. He drives 15 meters around the circle to Maple Street. If the traffic circle is a perfect circle with a radius of 10 meters, at what angle is Maple Street to Elm Street?

    A)   172°

    B)   86°

    C)   46°

    D)   14°

5. Points B and C are on a circle, and a chord is formed by line segment $\overline{BC}$. If the distance from the center of the circle to point B is 10 centimeters, and the distance from the center of the circle to line segment $\overline{BC}$ is 8 centimeters, what is the length of line segment $\overline{BC}$?

    A)   6 centimeters

    B)   4 centimeters

    C)   12 centimeters

    D)   14 centimeters

Triangles

1. Liz is installing a tile backsplash. If each tile is an equilateral triangle with sides that measure 6 centimeters in length, how many tiles does she need to cover an area of 1800 square centimeters?

   A)   36 tiles

   B)   100 tiles

   C)   50 tiles

   D)   300 tiles

2. The perimeter of an isosceles triangle is 25 centimeters. If the legs are twice as long as the base, what is the length of the base?

   A)   5 centimeters

   B)   10 centimeters

   C)   15 centimeters

   D)   8.3 centimeters

3. Mike leans a ladder against his house. If the ladder makes a 20 degree angle with the wall of the house, and the wall of the house makes a 90 degree angle with the ground, what angle does the ladder make with the ground?

   A)   120 degrees

   B)   60 degrees

   C)   70 degrees

   D)   20 degrees

4. A square is divided into 8 congruent triangles by drawing 2 diagonals and 2 lines that bisect each side. If the area of 1 of these triangles is 32 square centimeters, how long is 1 side of the square?

   A)   16 centimeters

   B)   128 centimeters

   C)   64 centimeters

   D)   8 centimeters

5. An equilateral triangle is divided into 2 congruent triangles by drawing a line from a corner to the midpoint of the opposite side. What are the angle measurements for these 2 new triangles?

A) $45°, 45°, 90°$

B) $60°, 60°, 60°$

C) $30°, 60°, 90°$

D) $30°, 45°, 105°$

Properties of Shapes Answer Key

Area and Perimeter

1. B

2. C

3. A

4. C

5. D

6. B

7. C

8. D

9. C

10. A

Volume

1. A

2. B

3. C

4. B

5. C

Circles

1. A

2. C

3. B

4. B

5. C

Triangles

1. B

2. A

3. C

4. A

5. C

Congruence

1. Liz walks 1 mile north, then turns and walks 2 miles in a direction 42 degrees south of west, and finally walks straight back to her starting point. Bill sets out from the same starting point, walks 1 mile east, then turns and walks 2 miles in a direction 48 degrees south of west, and finally walks straight back to his starting point. Who walked a longer distance back to the starting point?

    A)   Liz walked a longer distance than Bill.

    B)   Bill walked a longer distance than Liz.

    C)   Bill and Liz walked the same distance.

    D)   There is not enough information to answer the question.

2. If ∡A measures 57°, find ∡G.

    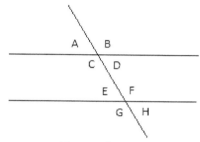

    A)   57°

    B)   147°

    C)   123°

    D)   33°

3. Triangles A and B both have angles measuring 57°, 78°, and 45°. Which of the following is true about these triangles?

    A)   Triangles A and B are similar and congruent.

    B)   Triangles A and B are congruent but not necessarily similar.

    C)   Triangles A and B are similar but not necessarily congruent.

    D)   Triangles A and B are neither similar nor congruent.

4. If ∡C measures 112°, find ∡F.

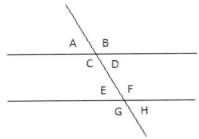

A)   112°

B)   68°

C)   22°

D)   158°

5.   A parallelogram is divided into 2 triangles by drawing a straight line from one corner to the opposite corner. Which of the following is true about the 2 triangles?

A)   The triangles are equilateral.

B)   The triangles are isosceles.

C)   The triangles are similar but not congruent.

D)   The triangles are similar and congruent.

Congruence Answer Key

1. C

2. C

3. C

4. A

5. D

Right Triangles and Trigonometry

Pythagorean Theorem

1. To get to school, Kaitlin walks 4 blocks north from her house, then turns right and walks 5 blocks east. How much shorter would her walk be if she could walk in a straight line from her house to her school?

    A)   6.4 blocks

    B)   3.2 blocks

    C)   6.0 blocks

    D)   2.6 blocks

2. A cone-shaped tent is 8 feet tall. If the radius of the tent fabric is 10 feet, what is the distance on the ground from the sides of the tent to the center?

    A)   6 feet

    B)   8 feet

    C)   12.8 feet

    D)   10 feet

3. Jesse rides her bike 2 miles south and 8 miles east. She then takes the shortest possible route back home. What was the total distance she traveled?

    A)   17.75 miles

    B)   18.25 miles

    C)   8.25 miles

    D)   7.75 miles

4. Point A is x distance north of point B. Point C is east of point B, and is twice as far from point B as point A is. What is the distance from point A to point C?

    A) $5x$

    B) $\sqrt{3}x$

    C) $2x$

    D) $\sqrt{5}x$

5. A triangle has angles measuring 45°, 45°, and 90°. If one side length is 4 feet, what is the length of the hypotenuse?

    A)   6.1 feet

    B)   2.8 feet

    C)   5.7 feet

    D)   4.9 feet

Trigonometry

1. Right triangle $\triangle ABC$ has leg $\overline{AB} = 12$ inches. If angle $\angle BAC = 35°$, find hypotenuse $\overline{AC}$.

    A)   20.9 inches

    B)   14.6 inches

    C)   17.1 inches

    D)   9.8 inches

2. Alice leans a painting against the wall of her bedroom. If the painting is 20 inches tall and is leaning at a 20° angle from the wall, how far is the base of the painting from the wall?

    A)   58.5 inches

    B)   7.3 inches

    C)   6.8 inches

    D)   18.8 inches

3. A triangle has perpendicular sides measuring 23 inches and 26 inches. What is the measure of the angle opposite the side that is 23 inches?

    A)   42.4°

    B)   31.6°

    C)   38.5°

    D)   41.5°

4. A right triangle has 1 side measuring 6 centimeters and a hypotenuse measuring 10 centimeters. Find the measure of the 3 angles in the triangle.

A)   36.9°, 53.1°, 90°

B)   31°, 59°, 90°

C)   42.1°, 47.9°, 90°

D)   Not enough information is provided.

5. In a right triangle, the side opposite a 25° angle measures 14 centimeters. What does the side opposite the angle of 65° measure?

A)   6.5 centimeters

B)   18 centimeters

C)   28 centimeters

D)   30 centimeters

6. A triangle consists of points X, Y, and Z. If sides $\overline{YZ}$ and $\overline{ZX}$ are perpendicular, angle $\angle YXZ = 17°$, and side $\overline{YZ} = 3$ inches, find the lengths of sides $\overline{ZX}$ and $\overline{XY}$.

A) $\overline{ZX} = 10.3$ inches; $\overline{XY} = 9.8$ inches

B) $\overline{ZX} = 9.8$ inches; $\overline{XY} = 10.3$ inches

C) $\overline{ZX} = 10.3$ inches; $\overline{XY} = 3.1$ inches

D) $\overline{ZX} = 3.1$ inches; $\overline{XY} = 10.3$ inches

7. The area of a right triangle is 24.5 square centimeters. One of its angles measures 45°. What is the length of its hypotenuse?

A)   9.9 centimeters

B)   7 centimeters

C)   8.9 centimeters

D)   10 centimeters

8. A plane's coordinates show that it has traveled 425 miles north and 378 miles east of its point of departure. If a straight line is drawn from the point of departure to the plane's current location, in what direction would this line point?

A) 48.3° east of north

B) 48.3° north of east

C) 41.7° east of north

D) 41.7° north of east

Right Triangles and Trigonometry Answer Key

Pythagorean Theorem

1. D

2. A

3. B

4. D

5. C

Trigonometry

1. B

2. C

3. D

4. A

5. D

6. B

7. A

8. C

Coordinate Geometry

Points, Lines, and Planes

1. The following points are plotted on a coordinate plane: $(-1, -1)$, $(-3, -8)$ and $(5, 11)$. How many of these 3 points are collinear with the points $(0, 1)$ and $(2, 5)$?

    A)   1

    B)   2

    C)   3

    D)   0

2. Mary runs 3 miles north, 4 miles east, 5 miles south, and 2 miles west. What are her final coordinates (in miles), with respect to her starting point?

    A) $(8, 6)$

    B) $(-2, 6)$

    C) $(7, 3)$

    D) $(2, -2)$

3. A square is drawn on a coordinate plane. If two of the corners are located at points $(-6, 14)$ and $(8, 14)$, which of the following could be a coordinate of another corner?

    A) $(8, 0)$

    B) $(-6, 0)$

    C) $(8, 28)$

    D) $(-6, 6)$

4. Which of the following statements is true?

    A)   Rays have two endpoints; line segments have a single endpoint.

    B)   Rays have a single endpoint; lines have two endpoints.

    C)   Rays have a single endpoint; line segments have two endpoints.

    D)   Lines have no endpoints; line segments have a single endpoint.

5. If 2 lines are drawn in a single plane, at how many points could these lines intersect?

   A)   0

   B)   1

   C)   2

   D)   A and B are correct

6. If line $\overleftrightarrow{AB}$ is parallel to line $\overleftrightarrow{CD}$, and line $\overleftrightarrow{CD}$ intersects with line $\overleftrightarrow{EF}$, which of the following is true?

   A) $\overleftrightarrow{AB}$ is parallel to $\overleftrightarrow{EF}$.

   B) $\overleftrightarrow{AB}$ intersects with $\overleftrightarrow{EF}$.

   C) $\overleftrightarrow{AB}$ may intersect with $\overleftrightarrow{EF}$.

   D) $\overleftrightarrow{AB}$ and $\overleftrightarrow{EF}$ cannot be on the same plane.

7. Which of the following is true about planes?

   A)   Lines never intersect planes.

   B)   Planes never intersect other planes.

   C)   Planes are defined by axes in 3 directions.

   D)   Planes are defined by axes in 2 directions.

8. A line segment has endpoints $(-4, 8)$ and $(1, 8)$. Which of the following is true of this line segment?

   A)   The line segment is parallel to the y-axis.

   B)   The line segment intersects the x-axis.

   C)   The line segment is parallel to the x-axis.

   D)   The line segment intersects the origin.

9. Lines $\overleftrightarrow{MN}$ and $\overleftrightarrow{OP}$ both pass through the point $(1, 2)$. Which of the following is true about lines $\overleftrightarrow{MN}$ and $\overleftrightarrow{OP}$?

A) The lines must be in the same plane.

B) The lines may be in the same plane.

C) The lines are parallel.

D) The lines must be in perpendicular planes.

10. Which of the following is true?

A) If 2 points lie on a plane, the line connecting those points lies on the same plane.

B) If 2 points lie on a plane, the line connecting those points intersects that plane.

C) If 2 points lie on a plane, the line connecting those points lies on a perpendicular plane.

D) If 2 lines lie on a plane, the lines are parallel.

The Distance and Midpoint Formulas

1. What is the length of the line segment formed by connecting the points $(3, 4)$ and $(-1, -12)$?

A) 16

B) 20

C) 8.2

D) 16.5

2. A line segment is formed by connecting the points $(-3, 15)$ and $(6, -9)$. What is the midpoint of this segment?

A) $(4.5, 12)$

B) $(1.5, 3)$

C) $(4.5, -3)$

D) $(1.5, 12)$

3. The midpoint of a line segment is located at $(1, 2)$. If the line segment is 18 units long, which of the following could be the coordinates for the endpoints?

A) $(19, 20)$ and $(-17, -16)$

B) $(10, 11)$ and $(-8, -7)$

C) $(4, 2)$ and $(-14, 2)$

D) $(10, 2)$ and $(-8, 2)$

Parallel and Perpendicular Lines

1. If l_1 is perpendicular to l_2 and the equation of l_1 is $y = 2.5x - 3$, what is the slope of the line l_2?

A) -2.5

B) 0.4

C) -0.4

D) 0.33

2. Find the slope of a line parallel to the line given by the equation $3y - 1 = 2x$.

A) $\frac{2}{3}$

B) $1\frac{1}{2}$

C) $-1\frac{1}{2}$

D) $\frac{1}{3}$

3. The lines l_1 and l_2 are perpendicular. If l_2 intersects l_3 at a $30°$ angle, at what angle does l_1 intersect l_3?

A) $30°$

B) $60°$

C) $90°$

D) $150°$

4. The lines l_1 and l_2 are parallel. If the slope of l_1 is equal to $\frac{3+x}{2}$ and the slope of l_2 is equal to $\frac{2+x}{4}$, what is the value of x?

A) 1.25

B) -2

C) 0.25

D) -4

5. Line l_A is perpendicular to line l_B and line l_C is parallel to line l_D. If l_A intersects l_C at a 15° angle, at what angle does l_B intersect l_D?

A) 15°

B) 75°

C) 165°

D) 90°

Coordinate Geometry Answer Key

Points, Lines, and Planes

1. B

2. D

3. A

4. C

5. D

6. B

7. D

8. C

9. B

10. A

The Distance and Midpoint Formulas

1. D

2. B

3. D

Parallel and Perpendicular Lines

1. C

2. A

3. B

4. D

5. B

Probability

Probability of a Single Event

1. What is the probability of selecting a queen of hearts or a queen of diamonds from a normal deck of 52 playing cards?

   A) $\dfrac{1}{2704}$

   B) $\dfrac{1}{104}$

   C) $\dfrac{1}{26}$

   D) $\dfrac{1}{52}$

2. There are 3 red, 4 blue, and 6 black marbles in a bag. When Carlos reaches into the bag and selects a marble without looking, what are the chances that he will select a black marble?

   A) 0.46

   B) 0.86

   C) 0.31

   D) 0.23

3. Winning a raffle depends on how many raffle tickets an individual buys, and how many tickets are bought in total. If someone who buys two tickets has a 0.004 chance of winning, how many tickets were bought in total?

   A) 600 tickets

   B) 25 tickets

   C) 500 tickets

   D) 250 tickets

4. A hotel has 200 rooms. Some of them have 2 full beds, and the rest have 1 queen bed. If the probability of getting a room with 2 full beds is 65%, how many rooms have 1 queen bed?

   A) 50 rooms

   B) 70 rooms

   C) 130 rooms

   D) 135 rooms

5. If a person glances at a clock at a random time, what is the probability that the minute hand will be between the 12 and the 3?

A) 0.25

B) 0.3

C) 0.8

D) 0.4

Conditional Probability

1. You draw 2 playing cards from a normal 52 card deck without replacing any cards. What is the probability of drawing 2 queens?

A) $\frac{1}{289}$

B) $\frac{1}{221}$

C) $\frac{1}{26}$

D) $\frac{1}{169}$

2. A telemarketer randomly selects a phone number to call. What is the probability that the phone number will end with an odd number or a 4?

A) 0

B) $\frac{1}{2}$

C) $\frac{2}{3}$

D) $\frac{3}{5}$

3. What is the probability of drawing a playing card that is either an ace or a spade from a normal 52 card deck?

A) $\frac{17}{52}$

B) $\frac{9}{52}$

C) $\frac{4}{13}$

D) $\frac{1}{4}$

4. On an airplane, there are 2 window seats, 2 aisle seats, and 1 middle seat per row (each row sits 3 people on one side of the aisle and 2 people on the opposite side). Two friends have requested to be seated in the same row. What is the probability that both friends will be assigned to aisle seats?

A)   8.2%

B)   2.0%

C)   4.8%

D)   4.1%

Probability Answer Key

Probability of a Single Event

1. C

2. A

3. C

4. B

5. A

Conditional Probability

1. B

2. D

3. C

4. C

Graphs and Charts

1. Consider the bar graph below. Which of the following would be an appropriate title for this graph?

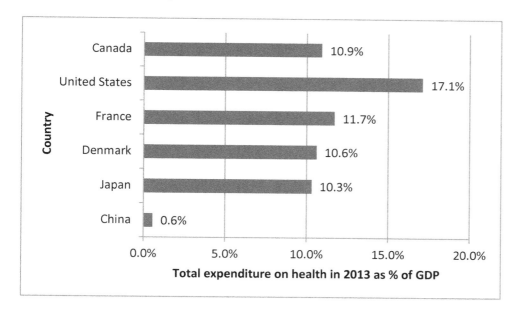

A)   Average Annual Expenditures as Percent of GDP by Country

B)   National Health Expenditures in 2013 as Percent of GDP

C)   National GDP as Percent of Total Health Expenditure by Country in 2013

D)   Total Health Expenditure per Capita in 2013 by Country

2. Consider the bar graph below. Between which two consecutive months did Sam see the largest percent difference in net income?

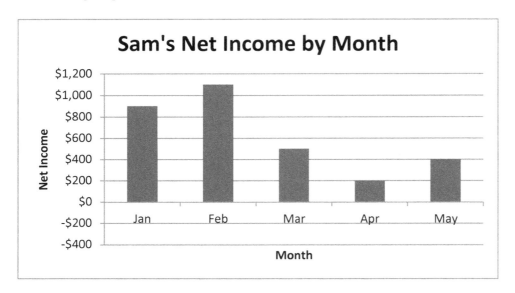

A) January to February

B) February to March

C) March to April

D) April to May

3. Consider the bar graph below. How much more money was made in sales in May than in April?

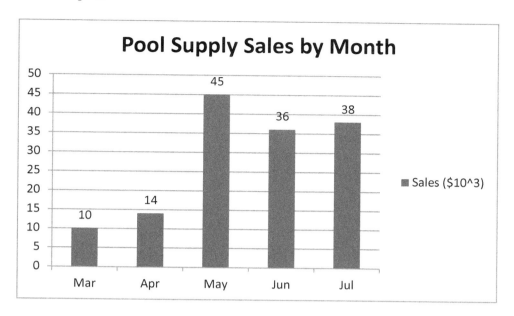

A) $45,000

B) $31

C) $59

D) $31,000

4. In a survey, high school students were asked to respond to the statement *movies are more entertaining than books*. Their responses are depicted in the pie chart below. Which of the following is true about the responses?

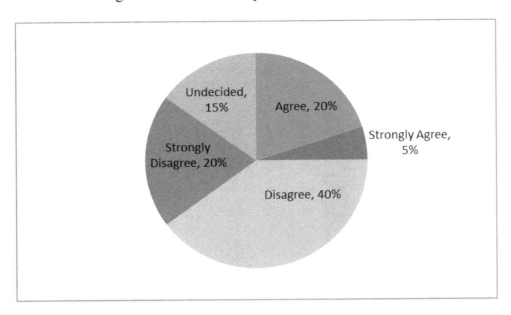

A) The majority of respondents agree or are undecided.

B) Equal numbers of respondents agree and disagree.

C) The majority of respondents disagree.

D) Of those respondents who agree with the statement, one third of them strongly agree.

5. The students of a high school's graduating class each enrolled in one of 4 types of universities: small private, large private, small public, and large public, as depicted in the pie chart below. Of the students who enrolled in a public university, what percentage enrolled in a small public university?

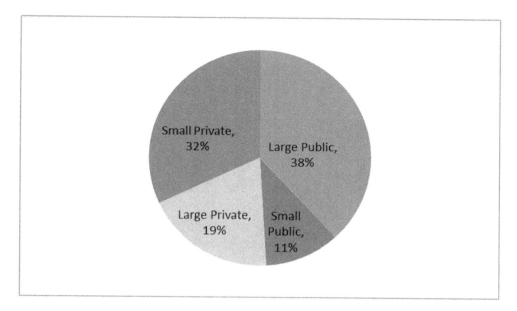

A)   29%

B)   22%

C)   27%

D)   11%

6. The pie chart below shows the number of children per family in a sample of families. If there were 60 families sampled, how many families had 2 or fewer children?

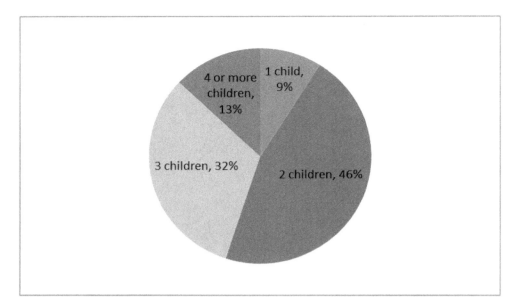

A) 33 families

B) 55 families

C) 28 families

D) 5 families

7. Consider the average height chart below for girls ages 1 to 16. What is the approximate change in height from age 4 to age 8?

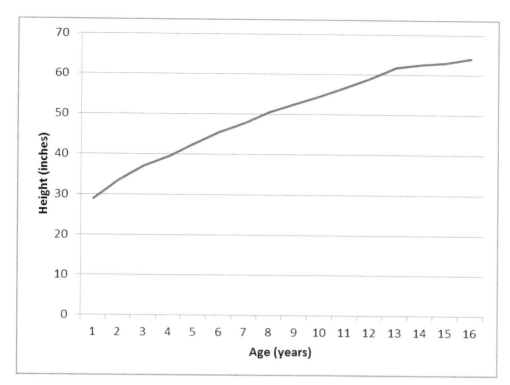

A) 10%

B) 50 inches

C) 10 inches

D) 125%

7. Consider the chart shown below for cumulative snowfall during a blizzard. During which period of time was the rate of snowfall the fastest?

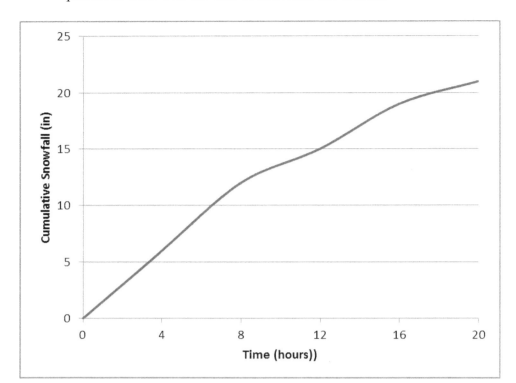

A) 0 to 4 hours

B) 8 to 12 hours

C) 12 to 16 hours

D) 12 to 20 hours

8. The graph below shows the cumulative distance covered by a car during a road trip. What is the average driving speed during the 5th hour of driving?

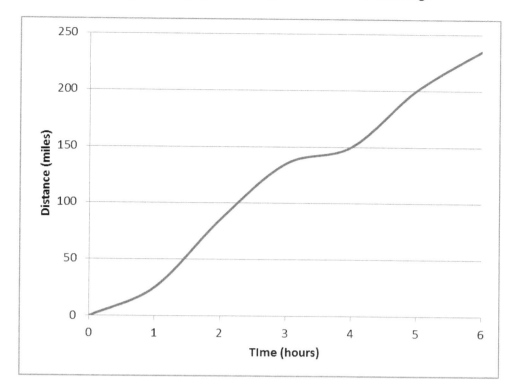

A)   200 miles per hour

B)   40 miles per hour

C)   45 miles per hour

D)   50 miles per hour

9.   The histogram below shows the distribution of students' birthdays. Which of the following is a flaw in this histogram?

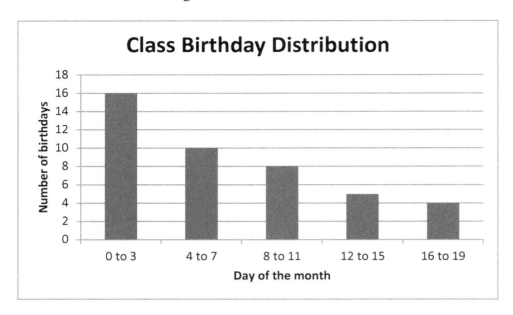

A)   Data points are grouped together instead of on a continuous *x*-axis.

B)   The bars do not add up to 100, therefore there must be an error.

C)   The last interval is larger than the previous 5 intervals.

D)   The number of students should be on the *x*-axis instead of on the *y*-axis.

9. The histogram below shows the number of customers visiting a shop throughout the course of the day. Which of the following is true?

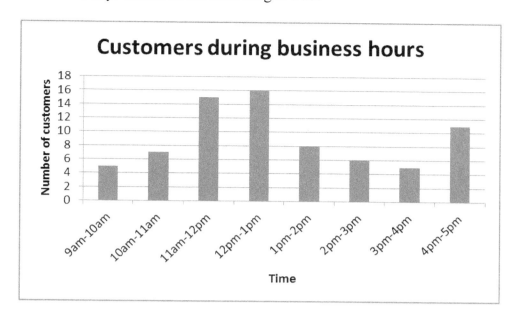

A) More customers came to the shop between 9:00 a.m. and 11:00 a.m. than between 1:00 p.m. and 3:00 p.m.

B) Four times as many customers came to the shop between 12:00 p.m. and 1:00 p.m. compared to 9:00 a.m. to 10:00 a.m.

C) The shop sees the most customers after 1:00 p.m.

D) If the shop opened one hour later, it would see approximately 7% fewer customers.

10. The histogram below shows a person's visits to a doctor over her lifetime. From age 0 through age 3, how many times per year (on average) did this person go to the doctor?

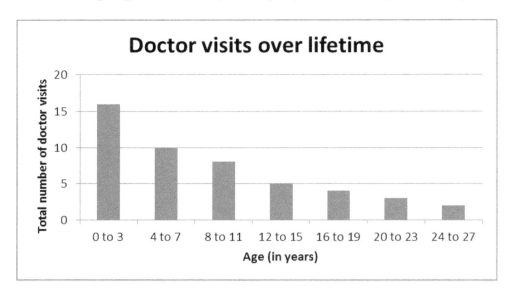

A)   4 visits per year

B)   5.3 visits per year

C)   16 visits per year

D)   8 visits per year

Graphs and Charts Answer Key

1. B

2. D

3. D

4. C

5. B

6. A

7. C

8. A

9. D

10. C

11. D

12. B

Resources and Help

You may have read through some of this book and thought, "Uh oh...I don't really remember learning that." That's okay! You are not alone. (It was the Math section, wasn't it? That's where most people forget material.) Not to worry, try these resources for additional help.

- **Purple Math** @ www.purplemath.com
  Purple math is a fantastic resource for intensive help on individual mathematic concepts. The website offers many extended tutorials in each of the subjects listed in the math section of this book. Practice questions are available here, so use them if you need more opportunities to improve.

- **Khan Academy** @ www.khanacademy.org
  Khan Academy is a great resource for math questions, as well as for tutorials related to individual concepts listed in this book. Simply visit the website and scroll down to the concepts you want to learn about.

- **Flash Cards**
  While flash cards don't work for most word problems, they can be valuable for improving your mental math abilities. Trivium Test Prep offers "brain trainer" math flash-cards to work on speed and accuracy in answering basic math questions. Flash cards help improve your mental math ability, as well as review concepts you must be familiar with for success on the exam. Visit our website under the "Product" menu to find the cards.

Final Thoughts

In the end, we know that you will be successful in taking the CHSPE. Although the road ahead may at times be challenging, if you continue your hard work and dedication (just like you are doing to prepare right now!), you will find that your efforts will pay off.

If you are struggling after reading this book and following our guidelines, we sincerely hope that you will take note of our advice and seek additional help. Start by asking friends about the resources that they are using. If you are still not reaching the score you want, consider getting the help of a tutor.

If you are on a budget and cannot afford a private tutoring service, there are plenty of independent tutors, including college students who are proficient in CHSPE subjects. You don't have to spend thousands of dollars to afford a good tutor or review course.

We wish you the best of luck and happy studying. Most importantly, we hope you enjoy your coming years – after all, you put a lot of work into getting there in the first place.

Sincerely,
The Trivium Team

CHSPE Essential Test Tips DVD

from Trivium Test Prep!

Dear Customer,

Thank you for purchasing from Trivium Test Prep! We're honored to help you prepare for your CHSPE.

To show our appreciation, we're offering a **FREE *CHSPE Essential Test Tips* DVD by Trivium Test Prep**. Our DVD includes 35 test preparation strategies that will make you successful on the CHSPE. All we ask is that you email us your feedback and describe your experience with our product. Amazing, awful, or just so-so: we want to hear what you have to say!

To receive your **FREE *CHSPE Essential Test Tips* DVD**, please email us at 5star@triviumtestprep.com. Include "Free 5 Star" in the subject line and the following information in your email:

1. The title of the product you purchased.

2. Your rating from 1 – 5 (with 5 being the best).

3. Your feedback about the product, including how our materials helped you meet your goals and ways in which we can improve our products.

4. Your full name and shipping address so we can send your FREE *CHSPE Essential Test Tips* DVD.

If you have any questions or concerns please feel free to contact us directly at 5star@triviumtestprep.com.

Thank you!

CPSIA information can be obtained
at www.ICGtesting.com
Printed in the USA
LVHW062223070920
665291LV00017B/1586